T0268366

Where the Shadows Dance

www.amplifypublishinggroup.com

Where the Shadows Dance

©2023 Dana Killion. All Rights Reserved. No part of this publication may be reproduced, stored in a retrieval system or transmitted in any form by any means electronic, mechanical, or photocopying, recording or otherwise without the permission of the author.

The views and opinions expressed in this book are solely those of the author. These views and opinions do not necessarily represent those of the publisher or staff. The publisher and the author assume no responsibility for errors, inaccuracies, omissions, or any other inconsistencies herein. All such instances are unintentional and the author's own. The author has tried to recreate events, locales, and conversations from their memories of them. In order to maintain their anonymity in some instances, the author has changed the names of individuals and places, and may have changed some identifying characteristics and details such as physical properties, occupations, and places of residence.

For more information, please contact:
Amplify, an imprint of Amplify Publishing Group
620 Herndon Parkway, Suite 320
Herndon, VA 20170
info@amplifypublishing.com

Design by Liam Brophy

Library of Congress Control Number: 2022920854
CPSIA Code: PRV0123A
ISBN-13: 978-1-63755-641-2
Printed in the United States

To every woman I've known who stayed silent about their pain, and to those still holding it firm, I was thinking of you as I wrote. I hope you find comfort here.

WHERE THE SHADOWS DANCE

a memoir

DANA KILLION

amplify
an imprint of Amplify Publishing Group

Shadow

[shad-oh]

noun

verb

1. partial darkness or obscurity

2. to be concealed from view

3. to be moved to the background

4. shelter from danger

5. a faint image, a trace, a hint of something we cannot see

6. a pervasive threat

7. an imitation of something

8. a source of gloom or unhappiness

9. an inseparable companion

10. protection

The life of a woman.

Do you see yourself here?

PART I

CHAPTER ONE
THE LAKE CALLS

I pad barefoot through the dark apartment, uncertain of my mission, knowing only that I can no longer lie awake in a bed that rejects me night after night. Despite the hour, the hallway is illuminated by streetlights, headlights, and neighboring high-rises. What am I to do with myself at this hour? Awake again at this hour.

Drawn to the windows in the living room, I stare out at the white-caps roiling in Lake Michigan. It's too late and far too dark for boats, but the light of the pumping station in the distance blinks red warnings, and a cold May wind whips outside, whistling against the glass. It's the only sound I hear, and I'm content with that. The silence of the night is uniquely appropriate, anything else would be an intrusion. Thirteen floors below, random lone cars cruise Lake Shore Drive, their headlights punctuating the night, reminding me that others also prowl in the dark at three a.m.

Naked beneath my thin cotton robe, I shiver, but I'm too mesmer-ized by the churn of the water to move. It's as if answers to my sleep-lessness and my aloneness can be found in its void. The insistent, angry

1

crashing of the lake draws me to it, speaks to me, haunts me. The power and force of the waves calls my name. If I dressed and stood at the edge of the seawall, would I succumb and allow myself to slip into its cold, dark depths?

As I stand at the window frozen in place, my husband is asleep in our bed, oblivious to my departure. Oblivious to the emptiness inside me. Oblivious to my distress. Has he seen a vacant look in my eyes? Has he heard the hollow echo of loss in my voice? Or is that too much to ask of him when he's only recently begun to see himself?

I won't stand at the water's edge and ponder my end. I won't stand on the balcony and wonder if I have the courage. This I know, but will I float away one day and dissipate like smoke from a candle flame because there is nothing left inside me?

I close my eyes, raise my palms, and lean my body forward, pressing myself against the glass, wanting something I can't define. I jump back, startled by the slick, cold surface that brushes against my nipple. The neckline of my robe has fallen open, exposing me, shocking me back into the room. Shocking me into feeling something other than the emptiness overwhelming me here in the dark.

Isabel jumps up on the ledge, rubbing her furry head against my arm, her soft purr telling me she's looking for attention. Is that what I long for too? Something as simple as attention? I honor her request. Then, with one more mournful look at the lake, I move to the sofa. I curl myself against the leather cushions and cover my legs with a blanket, a position and place that has become my middle-of-the-night reprieve. I lie there, feeling my body give way, waiting for my breath to slow. As I watch the shadows of life floors below me reflecting up, teasing me, dancing across the ceiling, I wish not for sleep but for dreams. I wish for the distraction of my obsession.

CHAPTER TWO
IT STARTED WITH BEER

It started with beer. Beck's beer. First, there was an empty bottle left in the garage, the sour smell of its spoiled remnants punctuating the air. On a rare occasion when I was driving my husband's car, I found another rolling around, clunking against the frame under the seat. Then there was an empty hastily tucked away on the top of a kitchen cabinet. *Wasn't there a full six-pack in the laundry room fridge this morning?*

I don't remember a distinct moment when I first wondered if my husband's heavy drinking was, in fact, alcoholism. Even then, I couldn't imagine a reality where addiction would wrap its tentacles around our marriage, refusing to give up its hold, draining us, challenging us, changing us both forever.

How could I have known?

First came the internal conversations: *Is it my imagination? That's more booze than I drink, but I'm a light drinker. It doesn't mean it's a problem. He's not slurring or stumbling or being obnoxious.* The questions floated through my head now and then and were dismissed as quickly as they came. Nothing I saw in the man who shared my life and my bed and my heart matched the image of a drunk, at least not the image I had. Yet the niggling thought that something was wrong danced around in the back of my mind, occasionally bubbling to the surface for consideration, as if it were a reminder of something I'd been meaning to do.

Life was normal. Good. Work, kids, a dog, a cat, a big, beautiful house—even a vacation home. Everything was as it was supposed to be—even better than it was supposed to be, better than what most people had, it seemed. There were no financial hardships or health issues or unusual stressors. Our marriage was solid, full of laughter and love, affection and lust. We shared values and dreams. We talked about business and politics and our desires for our future. We finished each other's sentences and laughed about that too. I was happy. We were happy.

Then one night he passed out cold on the floor of the family room, sprawled out on the carpet next to the fire in the wood-burning stove. I shook him, saying his name. I kissed the side of his face and nuzzled his neck. But try as I might, he would not wake, so I doused the fire and went to bed alone, fuming. We had never gone to bed alone, not even once, unless one of us was traveling. An hour later, as I lay awake in the dark, my mind twisted in annoyance and confusion and worry, he came in. The bedroom was quiet, lit only by moonlight. I kept my eyes closed, feigning sleep—still irritated but not wanting an argument at one o'clock in the morning.

"Bitch!" he spat out as he walked past our bed to the closet at the back of the room.

I froze. He'd never called me names, had never spoken to me with anything more than mild irritation. It was the booze. I knew that and didn't respond. I was still, keeping my back to him as he climbed into bed, and I lay there pretending to be unaware of him, silently process-

4

ing what had just happened. I listened to his breathing quickly grow steady and heavy as he fell asleep. And smelling the stench of the alcohol.

In the morning, I saw the foggy headache in his eyes and wondered if he remembered. He was quiet, as was I, but there was no time to insert a "what the hell?" conversation in between dressing, organizing backpacks, and arguing with my six-year-old over why I wouldn't give him Cap'n Crunch for breakfast on a school day.

Later that night after I put the kids to bed, I came into the family room where my husband sat mindlessly scrolling through the TV listings.

"What was that all about last night?" I said, sitting on the sofa next to him, watching his face.

He turned to me, his eyes tight. "Good question. I woke up on the floor and you were long gone. Why the hell didn't you wake me?"

"I tried. I shook you. Tried for ten, maybe fifteen minutes, but you were dead to the world. So I went to bed."

The annoyance left his face, but he didn't say anything more.

"I was talking about you calling me a bitch."

"What? I'd never call you that."

"Well, you did last night. You came into the bedroom and called me a bitch before you passed out again."

"I did? I don't remember that. I guess I was really tired. Sorry."

He had no memory of passing out or calling me names or even getting upstairs.

He brushed it off as nothing more than an evening of too much to drink, maybe too much stress at work. The incident passed, seemingly a one-time event. But it lifted the veil, placing momentary attention on a behavior that didn't match our norm.

His drinking moderated, and life returned to what it had been. We were a happy family with a life full of cherished moments: The look of pure joy on our oldest son's face as my husband taught him to ride a bike. Long bedtime reading sessions where wizards and magic fueled the boys' dreams. Watching the kids run our cocker spaniel, Bailey, around the cul-de-sac before he lost his sight. The four of us dancing together unabashedly one evening in the living room to Will Smith. My husband sharing his love of fishing with our youngest.

But the calm didn't last. It never does with an addict. Eventually, there was another pass-out drunk incident, and then another. There were more empty bottles tucked into places they didn't belong. And the signs, along with the worry gnawing at my gut, became impossible to ignore.

That my husband was an addict hadn't yet occurred to me. I had no personal history with the disease of alcoholism; I only knew the bad movie versions of slurred speech, stumbling, job loss, and car accidents. But that wasn't my husband. Nothing was wrong other than my belief that this level of alcohol consumption wasn't healthy—for him or for us.

When I first dipped a toe in the water, I was simply a concerned wife mindfully pulling his attention to his drinking, assuming that rational conversation on the subject could occur. He was an intelligent, loving man. There was never a thought that a frank conversation wouldn't be the answer.

"Do you really need another?" I asked. "You seem to be drinking a lot. Are you worried about something?"

And a short but rational conversation did occur.

"Yeah, I guess I have. It's probably this thing at work. You know, just stress," he said.

Conversation over. And things went back to normal, with no tension. His alcohol consumption lightened up.

I'd accomplished something. I was proud that we'd been adults about the whole thing, and I believed that would be the end of it. We had dealt with our first real marital conflict in a mature, balanced way. No fighting. No histrionics. Crisis averted. We were in agreement, as we were about so many things in our life.

The empty beer bottles no longer revealed themselves in strange places. He hadn't quit drinking—there was no reason to—but I saw no evidence his drinking extended beyond a reasonable two or three bottles of beer a night.

We fell back into our patterns, the ones that all marriages develop, of family and friends and life. We shared details about our days and our worries about the world. We celebrated each other's accomplishments and watched our children grow. And still, I looked at my husband with awe, filled with the love and adoration I had felt for him from almost the moment we met. Just his smile made me melt each and every time. It always had. And now my love was enhanced by his willingness to recognize that his drinking was causing me to worry.

I was so fucking naive.

Was it his smile or easy confidence, his quick humor or obvious intelligence that got me first? Likely it was a combination, as I can't separate one from the other—can't disassemble the package. It wasn't love at first sight, but it sure as hell was a silent "Oh wow!" We'd met at work. I'd joined the company just a few short weeks before he had, along with a contingent of new directors and VPs. We had been charged with revitalizing a retail brand that was losing market share, and we'd all relocated from around the country for this exciting new opportunity. All of that provided built-in reasons to go to lunch or out for dinner or to meet for drinks. It was new and exciting, ripe with possibilities. It was Florida.

He came into my cramped little office as part of a scheduled get-to-know-the-other-executives orientation, wearing a white mandarin collar shirt, tan pleated linen trousers, and a smile that made my stomach flutter. My first thought, after registering his obvious attractiveness, was, *Interesting. A guy who cares about clothes.* He was engaging. He asked questions, and unlike most of the men I'd come across at that level, he wasn't trying to sell me on his qualifications for the job he'd already been hired to do.

As I listened to him speak, I thought, *I wonder if he's single?*

In a matter of weeks, lunches here and there that appeared to lack an agenda became a dinner alone. We met at a restaurant near the water on a balmy evening in April. We dined on fresh, grilled grouper and drank good wine. Conversation flowed easily from our industry to our shared experiences of having lived in New York City to tidbits of our personal lives. He had relocated from New York and I from Wisconsin, and we both found the dramatic change of scenery in this new life was magical. He shared stories of his teenage daughters from an early marriage, and I shared a brief account of a recent break-up. It was an evening of easy laughter, long looks, and the hint of anticipation. After the meal, we stood in the parking garage next to my Honda saying goodnight, the Florida air still warm, the flush of attraction in our faces.

He looked at me, paused, and said, "You deserve to be happy."

I smiled and said, "So do you." Then I kissed him. Not on the cheek but a direct, soft, purposeful kiss on the mouth.

I'd never done that before, never made the first move. It felt strong and powerful and right. I hadn't planned it, but at that moment, I did what I felt. I wanted my interest to be clear. As I pulled back, I saw an expression that I couldn't quite interpret, as if I'd surprised him. I knew I hadn't misjudged his interest. He clearly wasn't displeased by the kiss, but I had caught him off guard. I said goodbye, got in my car, and drove home with the feel of his mouth lingering on mine.

I'd learn later that his expression hadn't been caused by my boldness but by my words hitting a place of raw reflection. I couldn't have known my seemingly innocuous comment would be profound to him, triggering an evaluation of his relationships and overall happiness.

On our next date, we walked down the long wooden dock outside the restaurant after our meal where we listened to the fish jump, felt the salt breeze on our skin, and stared at the moon as it glistened on the water. Then we stared at each other, quickly getting swept away in a rush of passionate kissing and groping that threatened to send us over the edge as our need to touch made us unsteady.

And so it was for us: fast, intense, passionate, lusty, heady. We hid our relationship at work and were married six months after that first date. Our fascinating new jobs had ended abruptly for all the new management hires after the CEO was replaced. And I followed my new love to Columbus, Ohio, for another new job. We arranged a small wedding ceremony, standing in front of the fireplace in our home, surrounded by close friends and family.

We settled into our life full of expectations and dreams, with the belief that "deserving happiness" was our future. The world was glorious and happy and overflowing with love. My husband, our marriage, and our connection all brought out something in me that hadn't been there before, or maybe I simply didn't know it was buried deep inside and needed to be coaxed out. I discovered a playful, openly affectionate side of myself that felt new and delightful. It was as if I was discovering the real me that had been hidden underneath my reserved outer layers. Love simply spilled out of me, uncontained. I couldn't resist kissing the back of his neck as I walked past him while he read or coming up behind him and putting my arms around his waist, pulling my body next to his for no reason other than I felt the urge to do so. It was easy and right—the way love was supposed to be.

Those words beside my car and that moment on the dock became delightful touchstone memories that we would revisit over the years, filling me with warmth. They were the down payments on our future being fulfilled. I adored this man. And would adore him still, even after he tore me to shreds.

———————————

Almost from the start, my love was something that left me weak-kneed with wonder. It wasn't just love; it was some new next level of emotion that rendered the word *love* inadequate. I settled on *adoration* as my descriptor. And not once did I question whether he felt the same. It was there in his eyes, in his touch, in his words. It was there in the small romantic moments we shared.

One morning, not long after we had moved into our house in Columbus, he left for work early, kissing me goodbye while I was still in bed. When I got up, the sun streamed into our white-tiled bathroom, and there on the mirror drawn in soap was a heart and the message, "I love you." I stared at that heart and smiled at myself in the mirror. This is what love was supposed to be like. Sweet, tender, and unexpected.

Birthdays, Valentine's Day, and eventually, any random Thursday, became surprise love bombs with unexpected bouquets of flowers appearing and cards or notes tucked under a pillow only to be found moments before sleep. Each small act professing our adoration for each other.

We spoke about how we wished we had met earlier. We could have—we had both lived in New York City at the same time, both worked in the same industry and, therefore, the same part of town. There was this sense of destiny about us. Destiny that we were meant to meet, meant for each other.

The external trappings of our life were things my family looked at in wonder and, at times, confusion. We had a stately three-story home with history and a beautiful yard close enough to downtown to not feel suburban. Our first trip together was to Italy where we explored Pisa and Florence and Venice. Eventually, we bought a vacation home in Florida on a canal looking out at Tampa Bay where the kids would swap out their jeans for swim trunks the minute we unlocked the door.

Midwestern girls from tiny Wisconsin towns aren't supposed to fly off for Italian vacations or off to their Florida vacation homes. My family had realized years earlier that I wasn't following the script they were familiar with. I'd eagerly fled small-town life as soon as the largest college I could find presented an opportunity. I'd lived in big, bad, scary New York City, a place where my father—having never visited himself, nor having any desire to—warned me not to ride the subway. I'd traveled all over Asia while working in the garment industry, sometimes living out of really nice hotels for months at a stretch. So my parents didn't really expect me to throw it all away and take up with a farmer, trade in my wardrobe for plaid flannel and shit-kicking boots, and decorate a log home in the woods with deer antlers and carved duck decoys. But they couldn't quite wrap their heads around what had become my normal either.

I was just this oddball my father spoke about with confused pride as he relayed my latest adventures to his friends and extended family. "Dana's off on one of her jaunts. I can't keep up with her." Although my life puzzled them, my parents were happy for me, because I was undeniably happy. They read it on my face, heard it in my voice, saw the glow in my eyes when I looked at my husband. My father, in particular, thought the world of the man I had married, seeing him closer to a peer than a son-in-law given our nine-year age difference.

My husband was thriving at work. Stress was present but manageable. He was doing work he loved, and I opened a gallery—a long-held dream of mine—using the severance money I had received when our previous employer had shuffled chairs on the deck.

But even in the best of times, booze threaded its way through our life, linking the extraordinary with the worry.

CHAPTER THREE
WARNING SIGNS

I imagine there were warning signs quietly flashing caution before we got married that escaped my attention—things I should have viewed through a suspicious lens that could've been a leading indicator of what was to come. But I knew nothing about alcoholism and couldn't see the connections that linked one incident to the next because my reference point wasn't based on reality. I thought of drunks in only the most stereotypical ways: slurring, stumbling, and yelling obnoxious things that embarrassed them in the morning. I didn't understand that the need for a drink could present without the falling-down-shitfaced part.

The patterns were what began to concern me. The pattern of passing out. The pattern of empty bottles tucked away. These incidents continued to happen regardless of how many thoughtful, teary, frustrated "honey, please . . . I'm worried" conversations we had. Talking never ended the drinking; it only moved it out of the spotlight for a while. But it always came back like a dandelion when you've only clipped the head—there are parts you can't see buried deep beneath the soil. And when booze came back, the frequency and intensity of his drinking simply increased, as if he was a teenager rebelling against the tyranny of parental rule.

One evening he came home from work late. I'd already fed the boys and was getting them ready for bed upstairs in their room under the third-floor eaves. The room attracted ladybugs in the summer and always felt warm and protected. We were sitting on one of the twin beds reading *Harry Potter*, one boy on each side of me, leaning against my arm. They were five and eight, old enough to read to themselves then, but our nightly routine had started years before, and none of us were ready for it to end.

My husband came into the room still in his suit, and I smelled the booze on his breath as he leaned in for a kiss. I saw the glassy look in his eyes and felt my body tense. *Working late? At what bar?* He said goodnight to the kids, then went back downstairs to change.

I read until my blood pressure felt steady, then tucked away the book for another day and kissed the boys goodnight. I quietly closed the door to their room. Whatever was going to be said, they didn't need to hear it.

"Where the hell were you tonight?" I shot at him as he stuffed cedar shoe trees into his loafers from a chair in the corner of our bedroom. Our dog lay curled on the floor beside him licking a paw, not even glancing up at my raised voice.

"I told you on the phone. I was meeting with my team." He didn't lift his head either. I imagine he assumed he could pretend his way out of telling me the truth by acting casual.

"Your 'team' obviously includes Heineken or Stoli or whatever the hell it is you're drinking these days!"

"So we went out for a drink. I can have a drink if I want!"

Ah, arrogance. When "it's no big deal" doesn't work, time to move on to "don't tell me what to do."

"*A* drink? Not unless that drink was a pitcher all to yourself. Enough. I've had enough of this. You need to see someone. This is a problem. A serious problem."

"You're overreacting. I don't have a problem."

"Well, I do!"

The evening devolved into ugly words, accusations, loud voices, and things we both wish we hadn't said. In the end, a bag was packed, and a hotel room became my husband's temporary home.

That was the first time I pushed for treatment. Whether it was a psychologist, rehab, or AA, I didn't care as long he started dealing with his problem. And it was the first time I had meted out consequences. I lied to the kids, telling them Dad had gone on a business trip, because they were too young for anything else. At that point, I also assumed that asking him to leave would be the wake-up call that shook his foundation. Surely, alone in a strange room, away from his family, he would see how thin the ice was getting and there would be change. In hindsight, it was ridiculous to have thought logic and reasoning could reset a disease that has neither, but I worked with what I knew, with my go-to tool: rational thought.

As he packed his bag and left, I recall thinking, *He can come back when he's stopped this stupidity.*

But the stupidity was mine. The arrogance was mine. I didn't understand his problem then. I thought it was something that could be corrected with a shock to the system, that the solution was more willpower or self-control than anything else, I guess.

My failure to understand our reality was one of the first broken threads in the tapestry of our marriage—a marriage I still thought was strong and unbreakable. My assumptions were one more small step on the road toward the overwhelming crush of pain that would come later.

Our separation lasted a whole week.

"This is getting silly," he said to me on the phone one night. "Can I come home? I get it now. I'll go to therapy. I promise."

Of course, I relented. He'd made the commitment I'd asked for. I loved him and missed him and just wanted my sober husband back. He returned, set aside the beer, and found a therapist.

After his third visit to the shrink, I was in the kitchen preparing dinner when he came home with an irritated look on his face.

"I'm not going back to *that guy*," he said, tossing his briefcase on the chair and taking off his tie.

"Why? What happened?"

"He asked me for money. Extra money. It felt creepy. Like he was blackmailing me or something. You know how this town is. Everybody wants to talk about other people's shit."

"Huh. That's odd." I stared at him, a drippy whisk in hand, confused—and not believing a word of it.

Concerned about his reputation, my husband was paying out of pocket to hide his treatment from his employer and the insurance company. He knew how the rumor mill at his company worked in this company town. Knew personal weaknesses had been leaked by loose-lipped staff eager to make themselves feel important.

And I knew how important his pride was to him.

"I'm not comfortable with him. I'll find someone else," he said.

I nodded, puzzled and wondering what the real story was, but I didn't challenge him. The method wasn't important, it was the result I wanted. The only thing I cared about was that he wasn't drinking. How he got there didn't matter, nor was it really any of my business, I thought.

Neither of us knew—really knew—what this problem was at that point. We hadn't educated ourselves. We didn't know what problem drinking meant or exactly how bad the problem was. We hadn't been forced to face reality—hadn't experienced enough pain yet. I'm certain the possibility of an alcoholism diagnosis had crossed my mind, but making a diagnosis was beyond me. Therapist number one likely hadn't had enough time to make a formal assessment—if my husband had even gone—and my husband wasn't inclined to discuss their sessions, so my armchair pseudodiagnosis carried little weight.

It also wasn't my responsibility to fix him. This is the stage when the insidiousness of the disease began to get entrenched in the DNA of my life, it became part of my being, altering me. But I didn't know that yet.

I just wanted this thing to go away, wanted it out of our lives. I'd done my job by pointing out booze as an issue in our marriage. The rest was on him. *You can take it from here, honey. Just try a little harder.* I was pressuring an addict to change.

It's right there in the Am I an Alcoholic? quiz. "Have you tried to stop drinking and been unsuccessful? Do you ever drink more than you planned to? Has drinking negatively affected your family relationships?"

Yes, yes, and yes.

"Now what are you going to do about it?"

What an alcoholic does—what my husband became particularly skilled at—is to hide it all.

Beer disappeared. It was too hard to hide all those bottles. Vodka took its place. It's colorless, has no obvious odor, looks like water in a glass, and it's harder to notice how fast the level of that great big 1.75-liter jug is slipping down.

But the body gives up its clues: The stale stench in the morning that even a shower and a toothbrush can't erase. The bloodshot eyes. The puffy face. The extra weight around the midsection.

I became suspicious when what I observed in his alcohol consumption didn't match the reality in his body. One morning, after he'd gone to work, I went into our bar area, which was in a small sunroom off the living room that connected to a deck off the back of the house. The space had been converted to a bar by the previous owner and was outfitted with a mirrored backsplash, an under-counter fridge, and lots of storage. It was also completely out of sight from the rest of the house. I opened the cupboard where the alcohol was stored, lifted out the jug of vodka, and felt my stomach churn as I stared in disbelief at the bottle.

It held a fraction of what it had when I'd looked just days earlier. He was drinking straight out of the bottle, chugging it down when no one was looking. When *I* wasn't looking.

The secret drinking had begun, and up until that moment, I had been oblivious.

The weight of what it meant crushed the breath out of me. Not wanting it to be true, I couldn't pull my eyes away. I scanned my mind for alternative explanations, but there were none—none that made rational sense. The bar area was out of view to everyone unless you were peering through the windows from outside. It was a place he could tip it back without discovery.

I made a subtle mark on the label—just pressing into the paper with my fingernail—to confirm what my instinct told me I already knew. Was this a daily event? How much was he really drinking?

With the children's bedrooms tucked upstairs away from sight and sound, our nightly reading routine had apparently become a daily opportunity for my husband to have unencumbered time with his new friend, Tito's. That night as I read to the kids, my mind was filled with anxious images of what my husband was doing at that moment and what awaited me downstairs. Some nights, he was passed out before I'd returned to the family room after the boys were safely tucked into their beds. Other nights, he managed to stay conscious a little longer. It became one of my gauges on the "how drunk is he tonight?" meter.

———————————

Gallery Hop was the big night at my store. On the first Saturday of each month, all the neighborhood shops and galleries opened their doors late into the evening. The Short North was both a creative and restaurant hub for the city, so hundreds of patrons would dine, drink, and shop. Lights, music, and laughter bounced around the happy throng as they wove their way in and out of the open doors whenever a display caught their attention.

In other words, it was a big-dollar night for store owners and a night for easy and effective marketing. It was an all-hands-on-deck event requiring enormous amounts of work before and after. New displays were needed, windows were designed, and the inventory needed to be a mix of impulse purchases and big-ticket home accessories that could turn a fifty-dollar sale into a sale of a thousand-dollar artisan table later. Staff needed to be trained on the unique features of the latest artwork or product and strategically stationed in the space, available to answer questions and to deter the occasional person intent on a five-finger discount. The Hop was a delightful rush of excitement and a massive drain on my energy, often triggering a migraine for me the next day, unaccustomed as I was to the crowds and the noise.

My husband, charismatic and outgoing, happily performed his unofficial role as greeter by chatting up shoppers while my staff and I dealt with what we were good at, speaking enthusiastically about the products we sold.

During one of the summer Hops—August, I think—my husband had shown up fairly early in the evening before the sidewalks were packed. The weather was perfect. The doors were open, and jazz played in the background. A table of things to nibble on was laid out in the backroom, positioned to entice people to move throughout the store. The crowd built quickly, and I was immediately pulled in, answering questions or explaining a process. As a shy, reserved woman, I'd never thought of myself as salesperson material, yet in this environment, my quiet nature stepped aside. I enjoyed the exchanges. I was simply sharing something I appreciated with someone curious about how it was done.

As I stepped away from one customer and moved toward another, my husband stopped me, put his arm around my shoulder, and said, "I'm going to step out for a little bit. I didn't really have time for any dinner. I won't be too long." He kissed me, and I went back to my job playing show-and-tell.

Sometime later, I looked up at the clock and realized well over an hour had passed. There were twenty restaurants within an eight-block radius. Where had he gone? I was too busy to give it much thought. I had two customers wanting to talk about quotes for custom tables from my favorite artisan, Bella Bella, and another eyeing a twelve-hundred-dollar floor lamp. When I noticed the time again, another forty-five minutes had passed. I scanned the room in case I had missed his return, but there was no sign of him. I watched the door and the clock, alternating between worry and agitation, trying to keep my happy sales face intact.

He returned around nine—an hour before closing time—waved at me, and as if nothing were amiss, immediately struck up a conversation with a couple who were admiring a mirror. I raised my eyebrows at him and attended to wrapping up any last sales of the evening.

After locking the doors of the gallery for the night and sending the sales staff home, he told me he had been stopped by a cop. We weren't yet at the stage where my immediate thought was, *Please, not a DUI,* so I just stood there looking at him in confusion, waiting for the punchline. Speeding? Parking violation? Neither. He had been questioned about public urination. He'd pulled his car into an alley, whipped it out, and let it flow. And a cop caught him.

"You did what?"

He laughed and shrugged. "I couldn't wait."

Huh?

The cop had been feeling generous and let him off without a fine. I stared at him, speechless as to why he couldn't get to a bathroom. *How far away had he been from my gallery?* But I still needed to tally the night's sales, take out the trash, and clean up someone else's spilled booze so the store wouldn't smell like a distillery in the morning, and that damn migraine was creeping in early.

Months later, I would think back to that moment and know that whatever meal he said he needed that night had just been a pretense for private drinking time. Whether he sat at a bar or drank in his car, I'll never know. By the time I realized the significance of his public peeing, too many other pathetic incidents had accumulated to dig back into this one.

———————

I wasn't yet familiar with the term *high-functioning alcoholic* as I grappled with my husband's drinking. I didn't have the knowledge or language to add a framework to the subtle variations of this particular addiction. Beyond the "gutter drunk" of unsophisticated movies or the lovable Otis on the old *Andy Griffith Show*, I had no reference point. The idea that an addict could exist in the world without the obvious external trappings was foreign to me. These are things you can't help but see—or so I thought.

I have a vague childhood memory of a whispered conversation my parents had when I was nine or ten. A friend of theirs. A car crash. One man dead. The drunk female driver was largely unharmed but mired in legal hell, and her husband was devastated. "She's an alcoholic," they said. Everyone knew it. I was too young to know what that meant other than to understand that this was a really, really bad thing to be.

Unspoken secrets often only find a voice after tragedy has struck, at least up in the Northwoods of Wisconsin. Everyone drank when I was a kid. Everyone had moments that led to a hangover or embarrassing behavior that they regretted in the harsh light of the morning. It was normal. I had seen my parents drunk, not often and not obnoxiously so. But there was the occasional occurrence of a concerned friend escorting one of them home safely, or a rare shouting match between them that I didn't understand but knew enough to assign blame to drink. It was just part of life as far as I knew.

Some fond memories from my own childhood experience included going to Sam's Bar with my parents after church or, more often, the American Legion. I was five, six, maybe seven, and my sister Sandy and I happily drank orange soda and were given a few dimes to play pinball games and bowling on a creaking old machine with a wooden court that rattled while my parents sat on a stool and drank beer with their friends. It was as much a part of their social structure as potluck dinners and snowmobile trail rides in the winter.

Although problem drinking wasn't a part of my childhood awareness, beer is practically its own food group in the part of Wisconsin where I grew up. The after-work Manhattan or old-fashioned was a ritual for my parents as they watched the local evening news before dinner at six o'clock. In my early teens, my father showed me how to splash bitters on a sugar cube, then muddle it before adding ice, a jigger of brandy, a top-off of Sprite, and a garnish of maraschino cherry—always the kind with the stem still attached. I felt grown-up and sophisticated as I delivered their drinks to them in the living room, but I never missed the opportunity to pop a cherry or two into my mouth as I mixed.

So I'm no prude in this regard, but surely I had missed some warning signs of a problem ahead. Something I should have been able to point to that flashed red. But if it was there, I can't place it. The line between drinker and future addict in my husband was too thin for my uneducated eyes. Yet I have had this desire to know. Wondering, I suppose, if my pain could have been averted.

Or perhaps his addiction happened later, evolving into a compulsion over time. I've never asked him. It felt irrelevant in my long list of whats and whys and whens. And it was likely a question without an answer, because to know that would have required a mind that was un-addled.

My upbringing hadn't prepared me for the role of booze monitor in my own marriage; I was ill-equipped for the job. But if it wasn't me, who? What else was I to do when I suspected my spouse had a problem? I had no backup plan, no convenient presence I could rely on for guidance or reinforcement.

Perhaps if I'd known more, read more, studied more, or talked to a professional earlier, I would have upped my game in figuring out my husband's disease. Perhaps I could have pushed us off the path that started with "this is concerning" and ended with "this is going to destroy us." Or I could've shortened the timeline or the severity or . . . ? I don't know. Something. The feeling still lingers that I didn't do enough. Didn't do it early enough.

But I didn't know. I didn't do that work. I didn't think diagnosing my husband's problem was required of me. Can I blame it on too much naivety? Too much "good little girl" leftover from my childhood? Too much life? Too much . . . what? I don't really know, but this vague sense of inadequacy has stayed with me as if I was supposed to have fixed it—fixed him—faster. There's the sense that my inadequacy needs to be forgiven. After all, this was my life too. My children's lives. What did I lose in the years while alcohol built itself into a being? Or was it something I was protecting in my life that I refused to see?

Feeling responsible is an odd, uncomfortable, yet very real aspect of being the "loved one" of an addict. Those who love an addict—whether as a spouse or a parent or a close friend—often take on the responsibility for finding a solution, assuming it's our job because we care the most, I imagine. Or perhaps it's just women who assign themselves this role, jumping in once again, expecting to find the solutions to family problems because we always do. It's not a fair assumption, I know. I haven't polled men about their self-imposed responsibilities as saviors. But it seems to be a distinctly, if not exclusively, female trait. Women are the family fixers. Whether officially nominated as such, it's the role we assume in all things. Why would addiction be any different?

Over time, as the obviousness of "a problem" became impossible to ignore, the research began—books, websites, any place that could help me find a framework that applied. But the surface examples of alcoholism did not fit. He drank, but he wasn't a drunk, at least as I saw it. Yet a problem existed even when the labels didn't line up squarely.

I also struggled with where I fit and what to call myself, clinically, in the discussion of the illness. It seems that there should be a label for those of us who find ourselves unwitting participants in the journey of addiction. We're wives and husbands, mothers and fathers, siblings, aunts, uncles, lovers, friends, but that doesn't define our roles in the disease or our roles in helping the person we love face and understand what's happening.

Or how they are hurting us.

Or themselves.

There is no "Hi, my name is Mary, and I'm an alcoholic" for us. Loved one of an addict? Father of an addict? Roadkill on the path to my husband's sobriety?

What are we other than sideline witnesses to another's self-destruction? "You're enabling. It's his battle. Let go and let God. Walk away with love." We're told all of these things. We hear the mantras of the addiction world repeated over and over as if they are supposed to make us whole through repetition, as if the simplicity of the catchphrase in itself is adequate instruction.

But our emptiness, if we recognize that it exists, can't be filled with slogans and punchy taglines. We plod forward putting our loved one first because the other choice is unthinkable. It's the disease we battle. Our needs will sort themselves out later, we think, if we're even conscious of our own void.

Yet we do have a role, often a pivotal one, in whether the disease ends in life or death, and it is supplanted by the necessary focus on the addict. Go to Al-Anon, we're told. Find a support group, we're told. We are accessories in the disease who must choose our own path lest we enable.

But this viewpoint undervalues our role, especially when we're the only people who truly know the extent of the problem. When we're the only ones with a vested interest in the outcome. Again, if not us, who?

A life was in my hands. The life of someone I loved with all of my being. There was no language around enabling or "the addict's journey" or powerlessness or setting boundaries that made any sense. It didn't fix him. It didn't fix me.

And most of all, it didn't stop the drinking.

CHAPTER FOUR
THE PRICE OF SILENCE

Ignorance was not my only problem. Loyalty, in the form of silence, was also an obstacle.

The deeper my husband got into boozing, the deeper I got into my own self-imposed bubble of silence. A loyal, loving wife doesn't talk about her husband peeing in an alley or passing out in the middle of sex while still inside her. She doesn't tell stories of turning away in bed, tears streaming because the sour stench of his drunken body is revolting. She doesn't talk about the fears that crush her.

Or was that just part of *my* loyalty pledge?

For many years, my father owned a tiny one-bedroom log cabin on a small lake in the town where I grew up, a lake so small motorboats were not allowed. In the summer, the property served as a family vacation retreat, and my siblings and I placed dibs on who got to stay when. The cold, murky water enticed anyone who fished, while a dock, a rowboat, and a screened-in porch appealed to anyone with more leisurely interests. The kids caught frogs or played lawn Frisbee. We grilled hamburgers and fresh corn on the cob, then toasted marshmal-lows for s'mores at night around a homemade fire pit near the water. We slept on pullout couches and bunk beds or sleeping bags on cots on the porch and listened to the call of loons.

My husband and I packed up the kids and drove up for a week one July, excited for the change of scenery and to see family. On the Satur-day toward the end of our trip, my sister Kris and her kids drove three hours to join us at the lake. Later in the afternoon, after they'd settled in, we took the kids into town for ice cream and fudge—a requirement of all northern Wisconsin vacations—while my husband fished from the dock.

He wasn't at the cabin when we got back from town and didn't re-turn for another hour and a half. Kris and I were sitting on the porch talking while the kids took turns climbing on the hammock in the yard. I could immediately see the buzz in his eyes as he poked his head in to say hi, and I knew what he'd been doing. He didn't come over for a kiss as was our custom, nor did he look me in the eye. There was a slight slur in his voice, and as he walked past us with a bucket of bait in his hands, he wobbled, a bit of the water sloshing onto the floor without notice.

I glared at him. I saw my sister turn to me, quizzically, but no in-quiry followed.

Later, as we managed plates of burgers, potato salad, fruit salad, and buttery corn from our perch in the small kitchen, my husband reached for a bowl, knocking over his glass of iced tea in the process. "Oops," he chuckled, and the kids joined in, teasing Dad while I mopped up the liquid. My sister's questioning eyes were back on me.

Later, when we were alone, she whispered, "Is he okay?"

I nodded and tried to summon a half smile, quickly changing the subject to something inane and nonthreatening. It was nothing but a minor incident.

I told myself I didn't have the energy—didn't want to upset anyone's vacation. He was on vacation too. But it was just another moment, one of so many, where I said nothing, guarding his secret. Our secret. Even when the person asking would never have judged me harshly, I kept my silence. I kept my loyalty to the man intact.

I don't remember a specific moment in my childhood that taught me to follow a code of silence. Family situations that would have led to hushed voices were few, but I learned it, of that I am certain. As the oldest of five, my responsibilities started young, and I thoroughly understood the expectation that I was to be the kid that gave no one any trouble. I saw it in my mother's harried face when family duties overwhelmed her. Heard it when she laughed at me, not with me, for repeating some stupid schoolyard comment that seemed sophisticated to me at the time. Learned it when my sensitive soul felt better away from any limelight.

And the world around me was no different. We midwesterners are not thought of as hotheaded, heart-on-our-sleeve types. Silence is simply understood as standard operating procedure. We aren't brought up to expose ourselves or make ourselves vulnerable. A practical, logical, sturdy, common sense lot, we don't have the time or patience for existential crises or the frivolity of therapy. Diligence, discipline, frugality—those are our innate Protestant values, our cross to bear.

We do. We are. We exist. We move on. We don't talk about it.

To place yourself in the middle of any story is to be vain. To call attention to something that should be kept private is simply not done. It isn't that midwesterners are without personal struggle, we simply don't discuss it until long after the incident has passed its pain point, or we refuse to acknowledge difficulties may require attention. Shut up and tough it out, you wimp. Unmet needs? Everybody has them. Talking about it won't change anything. Who cares? Bold, wear-it-on-your-sleeve emotion is for those with little self-control or reserved for times when beer has adequately lubricated inhibitions. Because then it, too, can be dismissed.

The prevailing understanding around tough issues in polite society is to be quiet, at least where I was raised. Don't air your dirty laundry in public. Difficulties are simply private matters to be dealt with inside the family. Speaking loudly and plainly about human weaknesses or pain inflicted serves no purpose or does too much unintended damage.

But silence is also the expectation forced on all women.

Be pretty and quiet and compliant and thoughtful. With an emphasis on quiet, please. And certainly don't complain.

The expectation of female silence is so ingrained in us we don't even know it's wrong until something happens or something breaks inside us, and we have no choice but to see it as an outsider does. Until we are forced to look at the face of someone we love while telling our truth and see shock or horror in their eyes.

Until we are forced to sit with the consequences.

And I have been as guilty of silence as every other woman before me. In what I assumed was marital loyalty, I kept quiet about my husband's alcoholism, rarely even questioning in my most private moments why I did so. In my mind, I was being respectful. I didn't cover for him or make excuses. I minimized his drinking on occasion, but there were no excuses to make. I didn't have to lie because life—the part visible to the world outside our home—looked fine.

I alone held the truth.

The children were too young. What our friends and family saw were the snippets, moments that seem insignificant individually. They weren't counting the bottles. They didn't notice his glassy eyes or his incredible tolerance for booze. His drunkenness rarely manifested in slurring or stumbling or boisterous personality shifts—unless the quantities consumed hit frightening levels. It was the low steady buzz he sought. Friends wouldn't have seen enough to connect the dots without digging under the surface. And if there was anyone else in our life who suspected, they, too, kept it to themselves.

Nor did I confide in my friends or family about my struggles. I played the role a loving wife is supposed to play. She protects her family. Those who knew the truth were a private, exclusive group: him, me, and eventually a therapist or two.

A high-functioning drunk gets through life hiding it all. He'd tough it out through the hangover and go to work anyway. He'd compartmentalize his drinking into time slots and places, so that outward appearances remain untouched. He'd rationalize that because he was still kicking ass on the job, he had it all under control. Denial was ingrained in him, and the disease was dismissed as belonging to someone else. Someone else with far more obvious problems. Success and charisma had layered their gloss on my husband, affirming him as "without defect."

Speaking publicly about my husband's flaws would be a betrayal, wouldn't it? I thought so. But was my silence about him or me? Did I stay quiet out of loyalty or out of fear for my own risks? I don't know. I didn't know then, and I don't know now. But the silence, the silence I chose, languished inside me like something rotting.

I'm certain I told myself I stayed silent out of love, but now, looking back, it reeks of weakness. A weakness that haunts me. A weakness that needs to be turned inside out, considered, analyzed, and put back into a new form. A weakness that makes me dislike myself and fills me with regret.

Holding in. Holding back. Holding on.

But why?

I would need to say it out loud.

I paused on the sidewalk outside a Michigan Avenue high-rise and stared up at the carved stone arch that crested the double doors. Buses and taxis buzzed behind me, and pedestrians sidestepped me as I struggled with my emotions.

I had no reason to be nervous, yet my heart thumped double-time in my chest as I gathered myself for the appointment I'd made. With a therapist. A therapist to help me navigate addiction.

Pulse racing, palms sweating, I looked up at the building and took several deep breaths. Why was *I* standing here on the concrete feeling like a shaky schoolgirl? I suppose I irrationally thought of his continued drinking as *my* failure. I hadn't found the exact right formula of love and concern that would get through to him. If I could, he would fix this. He would fix this for us. For me.

Or maybe I worried he just didn't love me enough to stop hurting me.

Although there had been fits and starts, stretches of time where I believed he'd turned a corner, it never lasted more than a few months. And now, many years in, after so many empty promises and broken dreams and returns to booze, it was abundantly clear his problem was too big for me to handle alone, so I'd opened a web browser and scrolled Psychology Today looking for practitioners with a specialization in alcoholism. It was one step up from the Yellow Pages, but I wasn't going to ask friends for a referral. And in the ways of a woman only seeing part of her problem, my thoughts were laser-focused on my husband's issues.

I was a lifetime away from realizing that a crisis was in my future too.

In the family-unfriendly ways of the apparel industry, my husband's career had pulled us out of Ohio. We'd spent a couple of years in New York while the boys entered high school, and we were now living what was essentially a weekend marriage. I was living in Chicago with the kids while he was in Dallas in a rental apartment for what was *supposed* to be a one-year stint and flying back every weekend.

And the separation had not been kind to either of us. He'd limped along on the booze front for a few years feigning acceptance, working through the stages of "I'll only drink with dinner," "I'll only have wine," "I'll only drink on special occasions." As much as six months would go by without any obvious alcohol at all, giving me the false hope that maybe he had this under control. Then something would happen, slip, and he would be back to passing out, back to hiding his drinking. Rinse and repeat.

But the transition and stress of this Texas job, and our awful lifestyle was negating anything that had felt like progress.

I could now hear the booze in his voice at night when we spoke on the phone—every night. I could smell it on him every Friday evening as he got off the plane, saw the puffiness in his face and his bloodshot eyes. But still, he kept it together at work, even excelling under staggering business demands.

I no longer knew what to do after having tried every tool in my personal toolbox. I assumed I simply needed better tools to understand what I was up against, needed different words, needed help convincing him of the seriousness of the issue. And if I could do that, I believed the problem would vanish from our lives.

But at that point, I also didn't understand that for him there was no middle-ground drinking. Normal social drinking simply brought the taste for it back into his mouth and restarted the denial of a problem.

So here I was staring up at a building in downtown Chicago, steeling myself to say aloud for the first time, "My husband is an alcoholic."

I arrived on the twenty-first floor and stepped into a small, empty waiting room. Surprised not to see a receptionist, I noticed instead a sign on the interior door that told me to buzz and wait. I sat down, and minutes later a sturdy, bland, midwestern-looking woman stepped out and introduced herself. I followed her back to a tiny room with framed landscapes that were barely a notch above the type found in airport hotels.

She sat in her chair, notepad in hand, gave me a kind smile, and asked, "What can I help you with?"

I felt my mouth drop open, but my brain was jumping ahead, running through the minutia of what he'd done and what I'd tried as if I needed to sum it all up in a sentence or two. Seconds passed while I stared at a stain on the carpet trying to formulate words.

"My husband is an alcoholic, and I don't know how to get him to stop," I choked out, tears already filling my eyes and constricting my throat. My body trembled as I sat, hands gripping my thighs. I had said it. For the first time, I had said it. Out loud. Now it was real. There could be no more rationalizing. No more minimizing or softening the label by thinking of him as a "heavy drinker" or "having a drinking problem." He was a full-on alcoholic. A drunk.

"Have you suggested a support group? AA?"

I laughed. Her question wasn't intended as sarcasm, but all I could think was, "Honey, if a suggestion was all it took, I could add a Dr. prefix to my name and set out my own shingle."

We spent forty-five minutes discussing the ways in which I had attempted to get him to his come-to-Jesus moment, including the "that therapist extorted me" episode. At that, she let down her professional mask and, with a look of utter disbelief on her face, said, "What?"

"Yeah, I didn't believe him either."

As the session wrapped up, she told me she "normally worked with the alcoholic, not the family" and repeated her suggestion of a support group. Then she asked whether I thought he would do better with a male or female therapist if she were to provide a referral.

But I didn't want a referral for him. Who he saw was his damn business! I needed help navigating and understanding his problem and getting him to see himself, not help telling him what to do or who to see.

It was only years later, thinking back to that session, that I realized she had never asked a single question about me. How *I* was doing. How *I* was coping. What support *I* might need.

"You are extraneous" became a new theme. My job was still to be silent.

CHAPTER FIVE
COLLATERAL DAMAGE

One Saturday morning, I sat waiting on the sofa, my legs tucked under me, my hands fidgety in my lap. Occasionally I'd catch a whiff of the Earl Grey tea I'd steeped and set on the coffee table next to me. The steam had dissipated as the hot liquid cooled, and I wanted a sip. Not because I was thirsty but because it would give me something to do that felt normal. But I didn't trust my hands not to shake. I didn't trust my ability to pretend my heart wasn't tight with dread over the question I was about to ask my husband.

There had been a night earlier in the week when my just-before-bed call to my husband had gone unanswered. We usually spoke first thing in the morning and just before falling asleep, wanting *I love you* to be the first and last words we heard. It was our routine. But my call was not returned. Nor was the second I made an hour later. He'd fallen asleep before, not hearing his phone ring, and got the message much later when he woke up, but he would always call eventually, even if it was two a.m. and he knew he'd be waking me. A short, "I'm sorry I fell asleep. I love you," was all it took. He knew I'd worry if that call didn't come. That night it didn't.

I spent the evening with my imagination running through every possible "is he in a ditch?" scenario. And I had a long list of bridges and semitrucks and concrete barriers pegged as possible explanations for his silence. Early the next morning, he phoned before he had showered.

"Sorry about that. I fell asleep. The phone was in the other room. I know you were worried. I'm fine. I'll call you later in the day. I have an early meeting to get to."

The incident haunted me the rest of the day, then the rest of the week.

It was the second time that month he'd gone dark at night.

So I sat that Saturday waiting for him to finish dressing. Waiting for him to bring over his cup of coffee. So I could ask the other question that had gnawed at my gut.

He sat down next to me. He raised his mug to his mouth, then looked at me. His eyes registered something he saw in my face.

"Are you having an affair?" I asked the question without preamble and said nothing additional to explain how I'd arrived at the need to ask. I couldn't. My chest was so constricted with fear of what his answer would be or an answer that I might see in his face that he didn't voice, that I couldn't utter another word. But I willed myself not to flinch, sitting as still as I could make myself, taking slow breaths to try to calm my body. I forced myself to watch every flicker in his eyes, every twitch or tick or distracted telling bit of body language I could take in as I awaited his response.

"No, of course not!"

There was a hint of indignation in his voice as he responded, but he didn't ask why I had posed the question.

I kept still. My eyes stayed on him, and my ears were trained to detect any uncertainty in his voice. I asked the next logical question. "Have you ever had sex, of any kind, with someone other than me, at any time during our marriage?"

Some instinct told me I needed to be specific. To ask the question as if I were an attorney in a deposition leaving no way to fudge the answer with some stupid, "Well, a blowjob isn't sex, is it?" if I later found out he was lying.

And I got a different response.

"Once," he said after an interminable pause.

He made the admission but couldn't meet my eyes as they bored into him, studiously gazing across the room at anything other than my face.

"When?"

"A few years ago. I was on a business trip in California. It was one night. Someone I met at the hotel bar."

"Why? Were we having problems then?"

"No." He sounded matter of fact, as if that would somehow ease the pain of the knife he had just thrust into my heart. "I don't know why I did it. I'm sorry."

"Have there been others?"

"No."

I said nothing else. He said nothing else. I didn't cry. I didn't externally rage. I was forcing myself to hold it together just long enough to leave the room. Details were unimportant then.

But it was one more sliver of my heart being thrown on the pyre of alcoholism.

He knew why he had done it, even if he pretended not to, and so did I. He'd been drunk.

I stood, while he stared at the floor unable to face me, grabbed my tea, and shut myself in the bedroom for the rest of the day, sitting with the pain. Struggling to comprehend his betrayal, my mind worked back in time, trying to pinpoint the exact moment he had desecrated our marriage and my trust. *Which trip? How had he come home and faced me? What do I do now?* I played out scenarios as the tears of gut-wrenching betrayal shook my body.

The mind of one deeply in pain and unsure of what to do is a strange and vulnerable place. Grasping for answers becomes a contact sport.

I couldn't talk to him. Couldn't even look at him.

But I had no trouble letting my imagination run wild, picturing a drunken night at a bar in a strange hotel and wondering who touched who and how.

Late in the afternoon, almost evening, the boys returned from an overnight visit with friends. Like it or not, I needed to face the world. I dabbed fresh makeup on my red, tear-stained eyes and tested my skills as an actress. My husband looked at me pleadingly as I walked into the living room, but I said nothing for fear of vomiting on his feet or heading for a kitchen knife.

The kids downloaded details of their visit while I forced a smile and pretended to listen, feigning excitement for the evening ahead.

We had a reservation that night for a family dinner at a lovely restaurant—a celebration.

The boys were excited to go. They enjoyed putting on sportscoats and ties, trying on the world of almost adulthood, eating food that expanded their taste horizons. They were in high school by then, old enough to have handled the disappointment if I came up with some excuse not to go to dinner, but I couldn't ruin their evening too.

So we all dressed and took a cab from our South Loop loft to the Gold Coast. We were seated at a table near the bay window of the

Victorian building. I ordered wine I couldn't taste and food I couldn't eat and spent the meal sitting silently, unable to look at my husband or my children for fear of collapse while the three of them chatted about the next movie they wanted to see and our youngest's next Model UN event.

I never asked what the boys had made of their mother's stricken face that night, choosing to shelter my children from this truth too. They certainly were old enough to have realized something was wrong and old enough to have heard an abbreviated version of the truth. But right or wrong, they didn't ask, perhaps sensing the danger behind the question. And I, again, chose not to tell.

Back at home, I got ready for bed, still saying nothing to my husband. I turned my back to him as I crawled under the covers, and the tears came.

He put a hand on my shoulder as I lay there, and it only made me sob louder.

"I'm so sorry. What are you going to do?" He couldn't say it, but he wanted to know right then if I intended to leave him.

"I don't know," I said, shaking off his hand.

It was all I could choke out. I couldn't think. I couldn't process his crime. And I sure as hell didn't want him to touch me.

This was the gift he gave me on my fiftieth birthday.

———————

Two weeks later, still confused and horrified and not knowing what to do, I booked a massage at a local hotel spa in an attempt to give myself a few minutes of diversion from the uncertainty of this new hurt. After the session, I sat in the relaxation room in a thick terry cloth robe, lavender essential oil floating in the air. A tray of raw veggies graced the coffee table. I was feeling warm and rubbery and trying to hold on to the feeling of calm. I poured a glass of cucumber water, then leaned back against the generous cushions and watched the boats on Lake Michigan through the eighth-floor windows.

Another woman entered the room not long after and sat on the neighboring sofa. She said hello, sipped her water, and settled back too. But she seemed uncomfortable with the etiquette of silence and quickly inquired about the quality of my massage as she had been a bit disappointed with hers.

I smiled politely and replied that my experience had been good, but didn't explain further, not wanting to break the calm of the moment with chitchat with a stranger. But she had other ideas.

"My name is Crystal," she said. "I live in Miami. I'm in town for a few days for a convention. I'm a psychic."

A psychic named Crystal—of course she was. I sat in my robe sipping my water and trying to keep the patronizing smile off my face while figuring out if she was going to shut up soon or if I'd need to make a beeline to my locker.

"Actually, I come from a long line of psychics," she continued. "My mother, my grandmother, my cousins, they're all gifted."

"Hmm, interesting." Definitely time to leave.

"Someone close to you has just hurt you deeply. Betrayed you," were her next words. "I'd like to give you a reading. No charge. I have a lot to tell you."

I stared at her round, shiny face and kind brown eyes, trying not to break down.

"You've read my situation correctly," I said, using formality as a shield. "Can you excuse me for a minute?"

I set down my glass, walked out of sight into the locker room, and lost it. I stood silently sobbing, trembling, my head against the metal door. I wanted to run. And I also wanted to know what she knew.

Wiping the tears and regaining my breath, I returned to the room but gave her no additional details. She had scribbled her phone number on a piece of paper and handed it to me. I stared at it not sure what to do. Not sure if I could make myself call. I was shaking and, for reasons I couldn't identify then, terrified by what she had said. And what she might say if I stayed one minute longer.

When I got home, I tucked her phone number away in a drawer but couldn't force myself to call her. I didn't believe in any of that. I thought it silly and fake, but I also didn't throw the number away. The thought stayed in my head for days, and I was still rattled by her comment. I had all I could handle emotionally with thoughts of *What do I do now?* Calling a psychic seemed just plain batty. I wasn't that desperate, was I?

The betrayal ate at me. It left me hurting, confused, and doubting myself. And him. But underneath the pain, I knew it was the booze. Booze was the demon that kept rearing its ugly head, tearing our tight-knit life into a weak mesh net. Booze was the cause of all of our pain. So I didn't leave him. Didn't seek retribution. Encouraging his sobriety became my mission. Understanding alcoholism, a new task. Ongoing therapy, a condition of marriage.

That was the "I'll only drink with dinner" stage, and the "let me try to do this on my own. If it doesn't work, then I'll go to rehab" stage when something as outrageous as a support group was suggested.

There was no dithering; he offered no excuses. My husband imme-diately found a therapist, coincidentally located in the same building as the one I'd seen just a month earlier and began weekly treatment. This time, no weird, stupid stories vaguely suggesting extortion were uttered, and I was again hopeful that this would be *the* thing. But I also still believed willpower was the answer.

And our life went on, but with additional shadows and fears and sadness in the background. The tapestry of our life was now marred by a new, deeper tear.

Those who have loved an addict know that their substance of choice creates a brain injury. It modifies the reward center, damages impulse-control mechanisms, and keeps the addict coming back for more. But our skills and tools as their primary support are limited. So we go about doing what we know how to do. We plead. We cry, beg, and push treatment on them. If they could only see how much they were hurting themselves and their families, they would fix it. If they knew how much they were loved, they would fix it.

These are our thoughts. These are the things we fight for. These are the reasons we stay.

We fight for them because they can't fight for themselves. We fight for them because we love them. We fight for them because that fight feels like the only thing standing between life and death. A life is in our hands.

One Saturday, a few weeks after my husband started seeing thera-pist number two, I was asked to join them for a session.

I sat on a brown leather sofa, my hands clenched around a wad of tissues, as far away from my husband on the couch as I could get. The clinician looked at me with a smile I assumed was intended to be comforting, but I was already clutching Kleenex and we hadn't yet moved beyond hello. He was a pudgy man with gray hair and a round red face. I imagined him in plaid flannel and elastic suspenders playing the banjo on a weekend side gig.

"So how does your husband's drinking make you feel?"

Do they really teach such cliched opening lines at shrink school? It sounded like he was trying to pull off the C-movie version of "how to be a therapist."

"Scared. Angry. Resentful. Hurt. Where would you like me to start?"

In a nanosecond, I had transformed from someone on the verge of tears to someone full of anger and sarcasm ready to punch my husband in the face and walk out.

I had entered the therapy office nervous and thankful my husband was getting help. But now in the room with this stranger, forced to talk about it, I was angry. *Why can't he just stop!* I had asked myself that question so many, many times by then. Intellectually, I knew that not being able to stop was the very definition of addiction, yet the question came back to me in that little office. I wanted the damn easy button! I wanted this hurt and worry to go away. I wanted my good life back.

But there is no easy button. Not even leaving him with his vodka and one-night stand would have been easy. I knew this was a fixable problem. Others had gotten sober. So I sat answering carefully phrased open-ended questions about how my husband's drinking affected me, while banjo-man watched me quietly and my husband tried his best to become invisible. Tough when you're six foot two and on the plus side of two hundred pounds.

We continued along with "my feelings" while my husband was forced into the role of listener shrinking into the couch until there were fifteen minutes left in the session. Then the big topic came up: his adultery.

"I understand the two of you had a tough conversation recently."

Understatement. Another tool in the therapist's toolbox.

"I asked my husband point-blank if he was having an affair. He said, 'No, of course not.' So, I asked if he ever had."

"How did he respond?"

"I got a different answer."

None of this was news to the therapist. I didn't need to elaborate. When I launched into my retelling of the "my husband forgot he was married one night" story, the incident had already been discussed—at least, from my husband's side. And this therapist was not tasked with concern for my emotional well-being.

I had been asked to participate to deliver the gut punch. I was the teaching aide. The prop.

Listen to her tell you *her* truth. Hear the pain in *her* voice. See what you have done to *her*.

I don't know what it felt like to my husband. To me, it felt like a pound of rock salt being poured into the open wound.

The following Saturday morning my husband returned home from therapy, pensive. He wasn't in the habit of sharing details of his sessions, and I didn't think it was my place to ask. But as we sat together over lunch on our rooftop deck on a beautiful July day, he told me one detail of his session. His therapist had described me as "collateral damage."

"Collateral damage in your self-destruction, you mean."

He nodded. "You're getting hurt because of my behavior."

According to *Merriam-Webster*, collateral damage is "injury inflicted on something other than an intended target."

46

Should part of that have comforted me? That I was "something" or that I wasn't the "intended target"? Although it wasn't said to me, nor intended to assuage my anger or frustration, I knew exactly what the therapist had meant when my husband shared those words. It was a kick upside the head.

"Buddy, you're taking her down with you. Wake the hell up!"

I knew enough about alcoholism at that point to understand that his drinking was self-destructive behavior, but I didn't understand its source. I didn't see the man I loved as having some deep, profound hole inside him. Although they were estranged, I knew his mother had been a teenager when she had given birth to him. Ill-equipped to be a mom, she'd left him to be raised by his grandmother. Tough, yes, but he never seemed to be carrying abandonment issues with him. He had grown up in a loving home with his grandparents and spoke fondly of cousins, aunts, and uncles he'd grown up with. The wounds of his childhood, if that's what they were, wouldn't have been obvious except for the alcohol. But maybe that was the point. It was another compartmentalization. "If I have professional success, none of that history affected me. How bad can this be? I can control my drinking."

At that point, I don't know if he was aware of the source of his wound. If he was, I suspect he wasn't grasping the depth of its impact. How can you when your brain is still waiting for its next fix? Whatever explanation he had fabricated, or been told by others, about his mother's abandonment was a story long ago accepted as fact and woven into his life story, whether accurately portrayed or not.

But it's hard to see the full picture of anything when you're only looking at one molecule at a time.

My label—collateral damage—didn't have a visible effect on my husband's acceptance of his status as an alcoholic. Perhaps it helped chip away a little at the hard crust of denial, but I'm not sure.

It decimated me.

The surprise wasn't that I was getting hurt unintentionally, that was abundantly clear. But to me, there was an underlying, but unsaid, message in that label. Your wife is irrelevant. This woman you claim to adore is unimportant other than for her role as a carcass on the side of the alcohol highway. "She's roadkill. You did that."

Those are the words that played in my mind when he uttered "collateral damage."

Could he live with that? Could I?

Understanding the intellectual argument and explanation for his behavior while at the same time being its victim is a tough place to be. The knowledge added to the spiral as emotions whirled inside me.

I was already living in a place where I flinched every time the phone rang when my husband was away. An unknown number would cause me to stare at the phone, afraid to answer, the pounding in my chest rising to a crescendo, expecting the call that would inform me he had wrapped himself around a tree or wrapped someone else around a tree.

Would my kids be in the car with him when he destroyed us?

At the time, he had experienced little in the way of consequences. Other than the fragility of our marriage, there had been no loss, no painful price to pay. No hard, tough-to-look-at yourself-in-the-mirror moments.

And I was still there, standing with him, fighting the fight for us, pushing, prodding, cajoling, yelling, crying. I was occasionally angry and resentful—often scared—but always loving him, unable to imagine simply handing him over to the disease.

Should I have left then? Should the revelation of his one-night stand have sent me straight to a divorce attorney? Would that have been the wake-up call he needed to get sober? Doubtful. However, it's one of the many questions that has rolled around in my head unanswered in hindsight. The truth was, I wasn't ready to give up. Nor did I see him as unwilling to participate. Our love was still deep and rich. Attending therapy was proof of something, wasn't it?

CHAPTER SIX
IS THIS THE BOTTOM?

I don't have the medical background to know where alcoholism fits on the difficulty scale; I only had the experience of a wife watching her husband slowly and excruciatingly poison himself with vodka. Suggesting that he was causing himself life-threatening harm would have been an affront to him, of course, denial being the alcoholic's armor, but an early death was certainly the eventual outcome of his actions.

Steatosis. Hepatitis. Cirrhosis. The signs of liver disease had already begun.

Addiction is an endless, complicated process, filled with relentless emotional turmoil. Love and hate. Compassion and anger. Empathy and fear. Nearly every human emotion plays out, occasionally at head-spinning speeds, for those standing on the sidelines of the train wreck. The lows razed my world into rubble, and the highs were my lifeline to another day.

I stood resolved to fill whatever support role I could because I saw no other choice. I did it for love. I knew I would do it until one of us broke completely and could no longer muster the strength to continue. I prayed with every ounce of myself for that strength in the silent moments in the middle of the night. I prayed for strength every time I looked at his face, love cascading inside me. I prayed for that strength when I hit the lowest of the lows, when I was looking down at his drunken, passed-out body or the ding on the car or the latest empty bottle of vodka.

And whether true or not, it felt as if there was only one thing standing between life and death: me.

To walk away would be to abandon my partner, my husband, my love to what seemed like certain death. So I went on. I dug deep and found the strength that he could not. It's a strength rarely valued in the throes of the disease. The addict in my husband wanted to avoid it, wanted me to just shut up about it, to let him be, and when I didn't, the lying and the denial and the refusal to face reality accelerated. My only focus was to end the self-destruction. His only focus was to refuse its existence. It became a cycle, a battle of wills, a one-step-forward-two-steps-back game.

It's a downward spiral that is a painful necessity in addiction. There is no healing if there is no bottom to the madness. But that bottom is itself elusive.

Like many before him, what my husband thought of as "hitting bottom" was, in fact, not.

I was traveling one weekend, exhibiting at a trade show in Baltimore known for its tough admission standards. I was excited to have the clothing line I'd started after the move to Chicago accepted, but my happiness was tossed to the curb when my husband was unreachable by phone the evening before the show opened. After a day spent in the exhilarating yet exhausting prep of booth setup and steaming garments and hanging carefully curated posters of models wearing my clothing, I was reduced to crushing anger. I was fuming because in a brief moment of separation, another occasion that was to be a celebration of my success was destroyed by my husband's need to drink.

I, of course, knew what had happened. I had no doubt that a bottle of something or a night at a bar had rendered him useless that evening when I was out of eyesight.

Early that Friday morning, just before the doors of the convention center opened and the first wholesale buyers were granted admittance, my calls were finally returned. "I've hit bottom," he said, not even bothering with hello. "I got a DUI. Spent the night in jail."

I was livid. And to be honest, glad it had happened. I remember thinking, *Maybe this will be the knock upside the head that gets through to him since nothing I've done has worked.* But I said little, unable to express my outrage in the middle of a goddamn convention center, minutes away from needing to put on the happy face of a saleswoman.

"I can't deal with this now," I said and hung up on him.

That night, after the show closed, alone in my own hotel room, I refused to answer his call. It was childish and petty, I knew, but I simply couldn't play the role of understanding wife. At that moment, I was done with silent outrage, but I had also never learned to fight. Good girls aren't supposed to have tantrums or boil over in rage. We are the rational, have-our-shit-together types who are supposed to be above all that. Step away, think it through, sit down and talk about it when saner minds have returned.

I didn't call him back until the next evening after I'd enjoyed a nice dinner with other exhibitors and a large glass of wine. I wanted an hour or two to revel in a strong day of sales, to allow myself to be excited by the buyers from a major catalog who'd expressed interest in carrying my line before I dealt with his issues.

When I called, his first question was about the calls *I* hadn't answered the night before.

"Did you not want to talk or weren't you able to?" he asked.

The question underneath was, "Were you just mad at me or were you with a man?" His jealous streak had imagined me so pissed off that I had bedded the first bloke I could entice. But that was about his insecurities, not any behavior of mine.

"I didn't want to talk to you. I was too angry."

It was his first public consequence. For a man full of pride and highly focused on his professional reputation, an orange jumpsuit and mugshot should have been the kick in the ass that made him serious about getting sober.

And it seemed to for a while, but my husband's consequences were short-lived, and the ego and arrogance of the addict quickly turned the arrest into something less. The violation had occurred out of state. That weekend, since I wasn't in Chicago, he had traveled to Florida to visit his daughters from his first marriage and had been arrested while driving a rental car. Some vulture attorney monitoring the arrest records called him in the cab the next morning as he returned to his hotel shortly after he had been released from jail.

A stable businessman, out-of-state license, first offense. A piece of cake for any attorney in the ambulance-chasing genre. "Just switch your car insurance into your wife's name, take your rental car business elsewhere, and in five years we can work on expunging your record," the sleazy lawyer told my husband.

Before long, the arrest quickly became something he set aside as not affecting his daily life. He retained his driver's license. "And do you know how rude that cop was to me?" This is how the protective mind of the addict works. "It wasn't me." They rationalize until they've twisted the incident into anything that helps them avoid facing responsibility. Because it's always about control for the high-functioning drunk. Control means no problem exists. Control means no change is required.

I, however, lived in fear of an accident, in fear that he'd kill someone, in fear of the lawsuits that could end anything left of our life. "How low is the bottom? When would he finally hit it?" These are the questions I asked in desperation, my pleas to the universe that day when I heard him disparage the officer that arrested him.

What is the end? What is the real bottom if a DUI isn't enough? The constant fear for those of us on the sidelines is that there will never be one. That there will never be a bottom so low, so deep, so painful that it breaks through the diseased brain to show them how much has been lost.

And if there was no bottom, there was no reason to stay. To stay was to watch death in slow motion.

But how could I leave when I was the only thing standing between my husband and his destruction?

But to stay would also be to deny the death that was occurring inside me. I didn't know that yet either.

———

There are no straight lines in addiction.

The path to addiction. The path to acceptance of the problem. The path to recovery, if there is one. The path for the loved ones of the addict. They are all twisted messes that loop around, fold back, double in on themselves, forming knots that can never be fully unraveled or marked chronologically on a timeline. But I didn't know that in the middle of the insanity. It was impossible to see where we were when

I hadn't yet grasped the full scope of the map because the detours and roadblocks and missing bridges were marked in invisible ink.

Each addict and each family member suffers through it in the dark, feeling utterly alone, braving a trail strewn with the debris of hurt. But the commonalities for those forced down this path are insidious: denial, lying, compartmentalizing, shame, guilt, fear, self-destruction.

Life, at least the boozy part, became a dance where worry and frustration would become too much for me, spilling over when fear or frustration initiated another tough conversation or angry words or— my personal favorite—stony silence. Then the alcohol would disappear for months, giving me a welcome but false sense of security until a small ding on the car or the stink of booze permeating his body in the middle of the night was so strong that I had to turn away from him in our own bed would tell me he was back at it again. Then there would be another talk and another promise and another game that I'd heard before. "I won't drink vodka anymore, just wine. I'll only have a drink with dinner. I'll only drink on special occasions."

The cycle was long and hard and had played out many times over years, but still, periods of time arose when progress seemed real and hope didn't seem to be a wasted exercise. I'd find enough hope to make me remember why I fought so hard for him, and for us. Then there would be a small lie, a therapy appointment blown off, and he would be back to the demon. But it would be uglier, hidden deeper. Because the one thing addicts of all stripes are universally skilled at is lying. Lying to themselves. It's the protective mechanism that keeps them from facing the real problem. The deep, empty, terrifying hole within.

And that is the real underlying fear. The fear of seeing the ugliness within. Because to face that fear means facing the ugliness in themselves.

It's hard to plot out something as tangible as dates to mark off how the disease progressed or when I felt as if it might be going into remission or what-we-tried-when. As I think back, I've marked its progression in my mind largely by the milestones of which therapist—his and eventually mine—was in rotation at the time. Or by the timeline of major crises.

His DUI should have made a big chink in the armor of his denial. At the time, he thought of it as hitting bottom. But no, it wasn't enough. It wasn't harsh enough, or big and damaging enough. Just use a different rental car company, pay your attorney, and switch the car insurance to your wife. It became no problem once the embarrassment had passed and the need for the next drink overwhelmed him.

These are the games of the alcoholic. Rationalization is as much a part of the disease as the booze itself. It was crystal clear to me that he was an alcoholic by that point, but I hadn't educated myself enough to understand how his disease might progress or to understand that the end was several levels of pain away.

The cycle of on-again, off-again, pleading and tears, promises and sorrow, anger and forgiveness, fear and thankfulness that he was trying was dizzying. And it also warped time into small incidents. I was so grateful for the sober time and so mired in hurt and fear during the drinking time, that it was impossible to step away and see that we were approaching two decades of this battle. And underneath it all, there was always big, bold, in-your-face, screaming with capital letters LOVE. It melted me and kept me in the fight, kept me unwilling to give up on this man I adored.

I could not walk away. I could not let the disease win even in moments of anger. Even in moments when I questioned whether I was contributing—not to his disease, I didn't blame myself for that, but was I doling out the proper consequences? Was I inadvertently pro-longing his acceptance of being an alcoholic?

One spring evening I took my husband out to dinner followed by a concert for his birthday. Buddy Guy was performing at the House of Blues. It was still cold then, teetering between winter and spring. We waited outside for only a few minutes for the doors to open, then walked into the small, dark concert hall. I made a trip to the ladies' room and returned to find him standing at the bar. Two glasses of clear iced liquid sat on the counter in front of him. I reached for a glass, as-suming he'd asked for water for the two of us. He stopped me. "Here, take this one," he said, handing me the glass farther away. I paused, stared back at him for a second, knowing, and took the glass. One drink was vodka, one was water.

He thought his game wouldn't be obvious. My stomach sank, and I turned away so he wouldn't see my disapproving eyes. It was his birth-day; it had been a lovely evening. Ruining it with the words that stuck in my throat felt mean on this particular day. So again, I shoved my disapproval out of the way.

I had gotten good at that.

This was one of his "I'm not drinking" stages. But that was just the story he told me. The reality was hidden. What he told himself when words and behavior didn't align, I don't know. Although I didn't un-derstand the full scope of his addiction, he didn't see addiction at all, not really. Even though other people had talked to him as if he were an addict and even after the DUI, he hadn't internalized it. Drunks go out for lunch and don't come back to work. Drunks get fired for screwing up. Drunks become the subject of whispered rumors at the office. He was none of those things and would never have allowed the booze to tarnish his professional reputation.

In reality, compartmentalization and control were fuel for his denial. And probably to some extent, mine.

———————————

What did I do when logic didn't work? When I felt, correctly or not, that I had few options? I pivoted.

At a time when I was still destroyed by my husband's cheating, devastated by drinking that simply wouldn't end, and at a point of helplessness in my on-again, off-again marital crisis, alternative spirituality came back into my thoughts. I'm uncertain how else to describe this world of symbols, mysticism, readings, and intuition. Nor do I know what practitioners and true believers choose to call it on a macro level. I suppose if you're deeply embedded in the viewpoint, it's simply your normal. Is a candle on an altar for a goddess wildly different from one surrounded by a cross and a photo of Jesus? It's heresy to some, I know, but I'm rife with agnostic tendencies.

I was frozen and confused about how to process my thoughts about my marriage after learning of the one-night stand, hurting in a way I had never hurt before. I was drowning in hopelessness and helplessness because I wasn't getting through to him about his drinking. And at a point when I felt I had no one objective enough to help me see clearly, I grasped at a life raft and made an appointment with a tarot reader. Yep, little old eye-rolling, get-that-woo-woo-crap-away-from-me, nonbeliever that I was, I went there. Could I get any more desperate?

I found my referral on the most reliable of sources, Yelp. I couldn't exactly ask friends in my immediate circle without them springing an intervention on me. On the list of things Dana would never do, it was up there with moving to Oklahoma or hooking up with a bearded mountain man or taking a cross-country camping trip on a motorcycle.

I needed a stranger. A stranger who wouldn't look at me with pity or horror or eyes that said, "Why the hell haven't you divorced his sorry ass yet?" Was I desperate? Absolutely. Even the prying, thought-provoking questions of an experienced therapist seemed out of bounds and unlikely to give me any comfort. I was already in an endless loop of wondering, *What do I do?* A therapist would just pile on more for me to sort out, more for me to feel, more ways for me to hurt. I'd been hurting for years by then. Couldn't someone take me by the hand and guide me? Was that too much to ask?

Skeptical, yet drowning in pain and willing to listen to anyone, I took off all my jewelry, skipped the designer jeans, carried a low-cost handbag, parked my Audi three blocks away, and walked into the shop. The deconstruction of my appearance was one of my "this has to be a scam" fallback tricks. Even the nonpsychics among us can call out a few accurate details after observing diamond studs, a wedding band, and a Balenciaga bag.

Tucked on a side street far north of my Chicago neighborhood, the warm, bright reception room was filled with beautiful crystals, amulets, and books. Potted plants sunned in the window. A light fragrance met me, but it had none of the oppressive incense quality I expected and despised. Soft, pleasant music played from somewhere in the back, and again my stereotypes were called into question. I'd heard more tortured chanting in a yoga class than here, where I seemed to think it belonged. After a moment, a woman I guessed to be in her early thirties opened a door to a tiny backroom and welcomed me in.

Her name was Amara. She was small and thin with long dark hair, delicate, beautiful features, and a kind manner; she met none of the flowy robe, unkempt hair stereotypes. This chick had cat-eye eyeliner! And she'd seen terrified, desperate newbies before.

I sat where she instructed and fought to keep my face and my body neutral. She handed me a deck of cards, asked me to close my eyes and repeat my full name three times, then cut the deck. The reader then closed her eyes and breathed loud and deep, shuffling the tarot deck as she did so.

She asked no questions as she laid out beautiful, colorful cards on the table between us in some order that was a mystery to me. As cards were pulled from the deck, some were moved around on the cloth-covered table in what I assumed was about interpretation adjacencies. Others were left isolated. Fifteen, maybe twenty, cards were fanned out, and I couldn't make sense of any of it. I was just glad to be silent and let her do her thing.

Then she opened her mouth and in a gentle, loving way, began to dissect me. My life, my relationship, the pain. It was all there in her words. *She knew.* And without hearing anything from me about my marriage or even that I was married, she said, "He's still lying to you."

The clenched, trembling hands in my lap were out of eyesight. I simply listened, my eyes on the cards, forcing myself to remain still and not to respond in any way that confirmed what she was saying. And I tried not to shake as she spoke. Through force of will, I made it through the hour, holding back the tears until I was alone in my car. Then I sat there, sobbing for fifteen minutes before I could collect myself enough to drive.

I'm not entirely sure what I was hoping to get out of the reading. I suppose I wanted a sign that it was okay to be indecisive about my marriage or a sign that eventually *I* would be okay. Part of me thinks I wanted to be told what to do and what the timeframe for getting out of the emotional hell I was stuck in would be—as if she could predict the future or tell me my husband would finally be sober if I could just hold on for six more months.

I didn't leave the tarot session with answers about what to do or how fast to do it or what his additional lies might have been, but I did leave comforted somehow, knowing that I possessed a strength and a resolve that would get me through regardless of the decisions I would eventually make. In other words, what didn't kill me would make me stronger. And that was prescient enough for that moment.

I also left with a belief that there are people who operate on a different system than most of us. People who possess a deep innate perception or sense of intuition, a knowledge, perhaps, that is beyond what most of us have developed. Or maybe the rest of us simply haven't learned to trust our intuition when it arises. If knowledge can be read in cards, so be it. Who am I to question how the universe delivers its gifts?

I haven't suddenly become a believer in angels or started consulting cards or the stars for direction on daily decisions, nor do I believe that every practitioner of "readings"—take your pick on the flavor—is honest and skilled. But one can say the same about therapists, attorneys, and doctors. Where I've landed is that guidance can take many forms. If it comforts, if it resonates, if it feels true to you, why can't it be? And if a kind soul can help me get there by interpreting pretty pictures on cards, I'll take the help.

And as it turned out, she was right.

———————————

I imagine the moment when the switch flips from casual drinker to addict can't truly be known. It's unlikely my husband could pinpoint when want became need. The alcoholic is always the last to see reality and can't discuss it with any clarity.

But that, too, is part of the disease. Even in treatment, unclear minds still rationalize the reasons why their marriage is in tatters, why their employment is hanging on one last chance, their lost driving privileges, the teary faces of their children begging Daddy to stop. It's always because of something else, someone else. It's another way to say, "I can control it. Really, I can."

Rationalization is the addict's religion.

How many go to rehab only when the world forces it upon them? Then they look around at their fellow boozers with pity, telling themselves for the umpteenth time "*I'm* not that bad. I've got this. I wouldn't even be here if my wife, my boss, my kids hadn't forced me."

Try all of them.

Although I never had to lie for my husband or explain away a drunken incident by declaring it "a rough day," there were moments when I bit my tongue.

I was on a video call with a writer friend late one Friday afternoon in July when my cell rang. It was my husband's secretary. She was supposed to pick him up at his rental apartment and give him a ride to the airport to return to Chicago for the weekend, but he wasn't answering his phone or the door. She called me worried, wondering if I had spoken to him. I knew instantly that he was passed out drunk.

His Dallas job was near completion, and an end to our long-distance marriage was finally in sight. He had left the office early, feeling no pressure to continue what had been eighty-hour work weeks. And, I imagined, he'd opened a bottle of something.

I hadn't heard from him, either, but didn't expect to until just before he got on the plane. I told her I would try to get ahold of him, hung up, and phoned, but I also got his voice mail.

I called the secretary back. "Just go home. If he misses his flight, he'll call a cab and catch the next plane," I said rather than telling her the truth about her boss.

At that point, all illusion had left me. He was a flat-out alcoholic, and I had faced that truth even if he hadn't. I told myself that telling her he was drunk behind that door she pounded on wouldn't have accomplished anything, but the acid taste left in my mouth from holding back that truth stayed with me and felt deeply wrong. Wrong because it denied my truth, my reality. Our reality.

Twenty minutes later, my phone rang. My husband had gotten his act together and was in the car on the way to the airport with his secretary, smelling like a distillery no doubt.

"If you've been drinking, don't even get on that plane," I said. "I don't want to see you."

"Don't be silly."

His words and tone were carefully chosen because his secretary was sitting next to him in the driver's seat. She had waited and tried again until the phone woke him.

Of course he had been drinking, and of course he got on the plane anyway. I was silent with rage and resignation when he got to our condo late that night, his drunkenness evident in his bloodshot eyes and the slight slur in his voice. Apparently, the solo party had continued midair. I'd long since learned not to argue with a drunk. Instead, I spent a sleepless night seething and settling on my response.

In the morning, I got out of bed, showered, and dressed before he did. It gave me time for a dose of caffeine and courage, and to get the stench of his stale, boozy body out of my nostrils.

I was sitting on the sofa when he emerged from the bedroom, the hangover crunching his eyes into dark slits as the headache and nausea engulfed him.

"You need to leave," I said. "I can't do this anymore. I'm done."

He hung his head and sulked, but he didn't argue. He simply turned back around, repacked his bag, and left, all while saying nothing. There were no more words. There was no case to be made for how he would try harder or do better. We were past bullshit platitudes and promises.

When I heard the doors on the elevator ding closed, I let out the tears. Then the body-racking sobs. I stayed curled up in that spot for two hours mourning my marriage. Wiping away the salt and the snot and feeling sorry for myself.

What I couldn't have known then was that that incident would be the last drink my husband would ever have.

When the tissue box was empty, I got up and opened my iPad, looking for the next Al-Anon meeting I could find.

On that gray Saturday morning, I parked on a side street in Lakeview outside Illinois Masonic Hospital and followed the signs for the auditorium once I entered the building. The halls were empty, as this wing didn't house the main medical facility.

I took a seat in the dimly lit, nearly empty hospital auditorium, separating myself from the others. Sobs still wrenched my body, and I welcomed both the dark and the isolation. If someone had offered me a blanket, I would have wrapped it around my head and shoulders, trying to sink into my pain like a child needing to feel protected and cocooned from monsters in a dark closet.

Having kicked my husband out only three hours earlier, I was still internally raging over an incident that was simply the last I could handle. I shook with anger and fear and helplessness and crushing sadness, grateful only for the darkness. I couldn't think about what I'd do now or what tomorrow would look like, I could only exist swallowed up by agony.

A group leader appeared on stage and, after a brief introduction, launched into a recitation of the twelve steps of AA. His words faded in and out as I battled my emotions. I wasn't in a place to hear him, not with the depth and understanding I imagine he expected. He spoke of powerlessness and God and detachment. Powerless I understood, detachment was an impossibility. But even through my anguish, I felt the scripted nature of the speeches. The mantras. The pep talks. The programmed language of groupthink seemed cultish to me, like I was part of some initiation rite for a club I didn't want to belong to.

After a while, he asked if anyone wanted to share. Two or three stood, taking their turns recounting a moment they felt strong or overwhelmed or to simply thank everyone for the emotional support.

What was the newbie etiquette here? Was I expected to stand up and declare my presence as the latest broken wife crushed by her husband's drinking? I suspect my tear-stained face and red eyes told the easy part of that story.

In the addiction world, the word *enabling* is bandied about as often as the phrase *higher power*. It's assumed that those around the addict are somehow facilitating circumstances that allow the addict to avoid facing their problems. By caring too much, by helping too much, by loving too much, *we* are part of the problem.

It was an accusation hurled at me and every other person in that auditorium who cared enough to push the person they loved into treatment, who cared enough to show up in support for the hard work of rehab. We sat joined only by our devastating love for someone with this horrid disease, feeling utterly alone, frightened, and nervous only to be told we contributed to it. There was no conversation about circumstances or our particular histories, simply the generic accusation that we must be enabling. It's as much a part of the formula as the addict needing a "sponsor" and the "one day at a time" mantra.

My first reaction was anger, then confusion. "I'm killing myself trying to help this man get sober. What the hell are you talking about?" I wanted to scream. I looked around the room expecting to see the others recoil as well but, instead, saw nods of acquiescence.

The concept of enabling didn't resonate with me, as they say in the world of enlightenment. That was not me. I pushed. I prodded. I begged. I pleaded. I screamed. I threatened. I cried. I didn't help him stay drunk.

But what did my silence do?

Would speaking loudly and clearly to our immediate world about our truth have nudged sobriety faster? No. I don't believe it would have. It would have driven a deeper, wider wedge in our marriage as his pride was also destroyed.

But what price did *I* pay for that silence? That's another question I didn't ask myself.

The thin line between silent loyalty and my own self-destruction had already been breached.

We were divided into sections of the room and invited to form small groups, then adjourned to meeting rooms next to the auditorium.

It was all women that day, I noted. Did men not join support groups? Too much vulnerability on display for the fragile male ego?

The group of women seemed to know each other, not in the "come over for a barbeque on Sunday" kind of way, but they knew each other's stats. "Her hubby has early stage liver failure." "She has a live-in boyfriend three years sober who just relapsed." "Her kid just moved into a halfway house after totaling the car and getting arrested." The women took turns sharing their weekly status updates, speaking about details that were both immensely intimate yet somehow not personal. As if the diseased part of their life was fair game, but they wouldn't talk about how they lived or loved or where else they might be vulnerable. That was friendship, this was not. This was their lifeline.

Throughout, I cried so hard I couldn't speak. I simply uttered, "My name is Dana, and my husband is an alcoholic," when my turn came. I didn't need to say more. They knew. They remembered this moment in their own search for support and gazed at me with compassion and pity for what lay ahead.

As the meeting ended, I was handed a stack of pamphlets and a book titled *How Al-Anon Works*. Did I feel any solace after the meeting? *Solace* is perhaps too strong a word. What I felt was relieved to have finally said my truth out loud and publicly, even if it was a weak admission at best. But another emotion hung there too—raw fear. As these women spoke, I felt the horror of realizing that loved ones of addicts were still struggling many years in. *Years?* Years after they had admitted the problem and sought help, they were still here. Still in pain. Still searching for relief. It was one of the most demoralizing moments of learning about this thing called addiction. Somehow in my naivete, I had only been able to see as far as the admission, as if "I'm an alcoholic" was the end game.

I spent that cold, rainy weekend alone on the couch, wrapped up in my blankie, reading the book I'd been given. I wanted some miracle words of comprehension or hope to seep in from those who'd been down this path. I suppose I understood more about the complexities of the disease after that weekend, but the takeaway messages of Al-Anon were flat-out depressing: Let go and let God. You can't fix him. Live and let live. Fake it till you make it.

Right or wrong, what I heard in those words was, "You have two choices, honey. Live with it and let him solve his own problem, or walk."

Neither was what I wanted. Neither was what I thought I needed.

My husband and I didn't speak for several weeks, nor did I tell anyone I had kicked him out, not even our children who were now in college. I couldn't accept this as our end. Couldn't yet face that reality, but I also didn't give a damn what he felt at that point. Rage and fear and indecision left me frozen, curled up in a chair, flipping repeatedly through the Al-Anon literature when I had run out of tears, as if some new insight would present itself or a half moment of clear-headedness would strike, giving me a glimpse into a path that would take me out of this hell, but images of divorce court filled me instead.

But the love hadn't left me. I didn't know how to set it aside, how to extract it from my bloodstream.

So three weeks into our silence, I got on a plane and showed up unannounced at his temporary apartment in Dallas. I called him at work in the middle of the afternoon and didn't tell him I was minutes away sitting outside his garage.

"I can't talk here," he said. "Let me call you from the apartment."

I sat in the rental car until he arrived, wondering if my marriage was about to officially end or if this would be the turning point in his disease.

He pulled into the garage on the lower level of the town house, and I walked over but left my overnight bag in the car. There was no sure path to how this conversation would go.

Oddly, he didn't seem surprised to see me. Had he been expecting me to do this, knowing that I had always been the one to reach out first? Had always been the one to make the first move when tension struck. His pride wouldn't allow anything else. But the forlorn look on his face when he saw me is something I can still see in my mind now, years later.

We went inside and sat on the sofa, the gulf of pain between us nearly impossible to breach.

"I'm sorry. I don't want to live without you," he said, wiping his eyes. "I'll get help. I'll go to rehab."

As he spoke and relayed his regret and his sorrow, I knew he was sincere. But he hadn't picked up the phone. Even the forced separation—and his ensuing hard realization—hadn't been enough to cause him to make the rehab appointment on his own.

I had wanted that, hoped for that, expected it even, believing the simple act of a phone call would be the sign I needed. But the emptiness I saw in his eyes told me he was still too deep in his own ego's spiral. And with that, another part of me died. Even kicking him out had not been enough for him to take charge of this himself.

The disappointment layered another hurt on the pile, but I remained quiet as he told me how he felt. There was no point in adding more shame to his burden. He had investigated centers thoroughly enough to know where he wanted to go, and after we talked and cried together, he made the call himself while I sat beside him.

Marriage or vodka. You can't have both.

He'd promised to go to rehab before, had asked me to grant him the gift of time to try to right this on his own. But like most newly aware, we had both underestimated the pull of alcohol, and those promises had not been kept. He was a man full of pride, and rehab without commitment was unlikely to be successful. The cycle of denial and addiction had never been strained to the breaking point, until now.

I stayed the weekend, then flew back to Chicago, believing that we had turned a corner. That somehow, in my ignorance, "treatment" would be *the* thing, the answer to every agonizing moment of our past.

It would save him. It would save our marriage. It would save me.

I had no other plan.

Ten days later, he was home, for good this time as the Dallas job had wrapped up. He had just come off the greatest, most harrowing feat of his career. His job had ended on a high with an achievement that changed our financial situation in a staggering way and had also driven him to utter exhaustion. But now he was back home in Chicago with me.

His days were no longer filled with meetings and phone calls and tense emails about whether the business deal was on track to close. His only pressing engagement was how to explain his upcoming month-long communication hiatus while he was at rehab to friends and family. His phone had been superglued to his hand for years, and there was no easy way to tell people he would be putting it on snooze for weeks. He wasn't about to tell them it was going to be confiscated at an addiction clinic. He decided to tell people he was "off to a spa retreat." It would have been a first, but it was a marginally believable, ego-salvaging explanation after the intensity of his recent business life.

Three days before he was supposed to go, we sat on the sofa after dinner, the TV tuned to some movie we'd seen before.

"Umm, I need a little time," he said as a commercial came on.

I glared at him, knowing instantly what he meant. He was trying to bail on rehab.

"Let me do this next month. I just finished . . . and I need a break."

I understood that he wasn't ready to process all the ugliness on the heels of his greatest career achievement, so I gritted my teeth and acquiesced, again.

A month later, the next start date came and along with it, some sorry bullshit excuse not worth remembering. This time delivered the day before his flight.

I stared at him, fuming, disgusted with his cowardice and with myself for not having pushed back harder a month earlier.

"I'll be back in an hour and a half," I said, grabbing my bag and walking out.

I didn't scream or yell or call him out on his broken promise. His stupid game was over for me. I was done. So I did the thing that would hit home the hardest: I left. No angry words. No explanation. I simply walked out.

I played to his jealous streak—not intentionally, but probably subconsciously. Unable to find words that hadn't already been said ad nauseam to convey in even starker detail my level of frustration and anger and worry, I bailed. I walked the streets for hours, drowning my sorrows at Starbucks and letting him imagine the worst. When I returned, he didn't speak to me, but he was packing for his trip to rehab.

The next morning, he got on that plane, angry and bitter. Angry at me for forcing him to choose.

But I didn't care how he got to rehab or how angry he was or how hard it would be. I got what I wanted. I got what he needed. I got what I believed would be the answer to our problem: rehab at an inpatient treatment center. But instead of salvation, the real pain came.

CHAPTER SEVEN
DOES SHOCK HAVE A TIME FRAME?

I remember the sunshine, the foreignness of the desert climate, and the desolate brown landscape. I thought I would be able to work on the draft of my first novel alone at night in my hotel room. My days would be busy, of course, with group meetings learning how to support my husband through his newfound sobriety. I had flown to California for Family Week at his rehab center. *May as well turn it into a mini vacation / work session*, I thought. Maybe I'd book a massage or a facial. There wouldn't be anything else to do.

I had been flying from Chicago to Palm Springs each weekend for nearly a month just so my husband and I could spend an hour and a half together during Sunday afternoon visitation. At first, he didn't want me to come. His anger with me for being forced into treatment and for his humiliation—having his phone confiscated, his bags checked for contraband, and being treated like a prisoner—was so great, he pushed me away. I came anyway. I needed him to know I was there, that he was still loved, that I hadn't abandoned him, that I was proud of him. Then, after he saw his inevitable future in the frail, yellow-eyes of those further down the path of alcoholism, he didn't want me there because his pride was too great to let me see him vulnerable. Again, I came anyway.

Not getting on a plane was never a consideration.

We walked the sprawling paths of the campus, noting the names etched in the brick pathway, or sat huddled together talking in a quiet spot on the second floor. He was practicing yoga for the first time in his life and enjoying it. Though, he was not so thrilled with having a roommate. He attended AA meetings, group therapy, and individual therapy. He was surprised at the empathy shown by his therapist, a woman. *Duh!* formed in my mind, knowing he'd only chosen men in the past, but I appropriately held my tongue. Each trip out, I saw in him a deeper understanding of his disease. As the weeks passed, he became a man who had set aside his pride and his ego for healing. The anger was gone. The "I don't need this" was gone. The "I'm not an alcoholic" was gone. In its place, acceptance and dedication.

Family Week arrived at the end of the program after the toughest work had been done and a deeper awareness of the price of addiction had hopefully been achieved. The reality of jaundice and liver disease, lost jobs and lost homes, broken marriages and broken families was all boldly laid bare. The magnitude of the countless broken promises and hurt inflicted had been faced. There was no hiding or self-denial allowed. It was time to design the plan for a new clear-headed life, to find a sponsor, attend AA, and commit to new behaviors once back out in the real world of temptations where old habits were close at hand.

We were herded into a plush conference room after saying goodbye to our loved ones, our faces full of worry, tears, or fears. Mine likely held all three as I clenched my hands in my lap, struggling to sort through the emotions bombarding me: fear of the unknown, of the vulnerability, of the risk of placing too much hope squarely on this one rehab stint.

Listening to the director's calm voice as he educated us about addiction and the history of twelve-step programs softened the anxiety. He cautioned us not to indulge in drinking ourselves over the six days of our program, lest it complicate the patient's progress. He spoke of self-care, enabling, the importance of providing support once back home, and the rate of relapse.

Like the patients, the visiting family members had group sessions. We, too, attended AA and shared stories of how addiction had ravaged our families—some of us for the first time. We sat in small rooms vibrating with our hurt, the hurt that had cascaded into the lives of those around us, and the hurt of the thousands who had come before us in these rooms.

I could hear the emotion choking my own voice as I spoke of my husband's DUI and the fear that gripped me when my husband was away, each ring of the phone from an unknown number assumed to be devastating news.

But there was comfort in knowing others understood and had been in the same place I was. Most had done this before and told stories of other centers and relapses and unending pain.

Those of us in the group who were virgins looked at each other alarmed. *Is this my fate too? There will be more pain, another relapse? Please, God, no!*

An awkward bond formed between us. We were strangers sharing some of the most vulnerable moments of our lives, but little was revealed of who we were outside the label of the "addict's wife" or "addict's mom" or "a dear friend of." We were thrown together to discuss our trauma but spoke of little else. There were knowing nods, heartbreaking empathy, and moments of wide-eyed shock at how bad it could be. There was a woman from Texas who told of her husband needing a fix so bad he drank lighter fluid. A husband who said, "I'm watching my son kill my wife," as he spoke of their child's heroin addiction.

There were moments I was grateful I hadn't seen the worst. And moments, alone at night, where *What do I do if this is not the fix?* dominated my thoughts.

Mostly, I held out hope, relieved that the years and years of effort to help him face his addiction had, at minimum, moved us into another stage and might, just might, bring an end to our pain.

But that's not how that week ended.

My husband and I sat quietly on a hard bench tucked away in the middle of a wide hallway on the second level of the main building—the pretty one, the one shown to the all-important donors. The one where the messy side of addiction is hidden behind expensive art and carpets and matching upholstery. Where the ugly side of detox and medical crisis is tucked out of view, away from eyes that only want to see success stories. It was the place we sat and talked each time I visited. The place he had scoped out for us so we would have privacy for our time together.

"We talked about that time, you know, that California trip, when I . . . ," he said.

He was telling me about his recent session with his individual therapist where they spoke about his one-night stand, sharing with me a rare level of detail about therapy. He liked this therapist. He trusted her, respected her. Each visit, a little less of his old armor remained. And that day he seemed particularly vulnerable. He sat on the bench, his elbows on his knees, staring at the floor as he spoke, regret in his voice.

"Have there been others?" It must have been his vulnerability that prompted me to ask. Betrayal never leaves you, rising to the surface whether you want it to or not. It has a life of its own and inserts itself when the skin of our hearts is thin and easily damaged.

"What? You want a number?"

And the world stopped.

As life changing as that moment was, it seems like I should be able to remember every syllable uttered after that, every action that followed, everything that was unleashed by the mother of all pain. But as hard as I've tried, it has disappeared in the torrent of agony. Those exact words, however, are burned forever in my mind.

My next memory is of fighting to control the wheel of my rental car as everything around me shut down and my body separated from my mind. I couldn't feel anything but revulsion. The road from the treatment center to the hotel became nothing but a pinprick of light that I strained to keep in front of me as the darkness closed in. Every ounce of energy I had was focused on the next few feet. *Hold on, hold on, just get to the hotel in one piece.* My body shook with horror, and waves of nausea struck as I inched along the handful of miles to get to someplace safe.

I remember a night confined in a strange place utterly alone, as alone and as shredded as I have ever been in life. Bile rose in my throat, and I vomited until there was nothing left. I paced my room for hours. I couldn't sit still, couldn't collapse on the floor. Like a shark, movement was the only way I could breathe. Sobbing, hysterical, unable to control my body, unable to rage or flail or lash out at my husband where he could see me or feel what he had done to me, I pounded the floor with my feet because it was all I had.

The human mind in the midst of trauma is aberrant. It lacks reason or purpose. As if I was locked in a waking nightmare, images and memories from that day have no logical connection. Strangely, I remember the layout of the hotel room. This one particular room, but not another before or since. I remember the placement of things. A king bed on the right, an upholstered chair and ottoman and floor lamp beyond it, a desk and dresser and TV on the left, a balcony running the length of the room. The sound of laughter from the pool three floors below that taunted me. But I don't remember if I ate or slept or how I got back to Chicago.

But I do remember thinking, *This is my reward for my devotion. His secret life.*

CHAPTER EIGHT
SELF-CENTERED PRICK

What happened in the days after his revelation? I wish I knew. I left that treatment center in a zombie state where my body had shut down all but essential functions, unable to process the lie that had been my marriage.

My mind moved into survival mode. The human psyche protects itself, and my psyche made me numb to everything. I moved through life on autopilot, eating only when my body demanded, sleeping only when my body could no longer remain upright.

Despite the time that has transpired since that day, the year and a half that followed is still largely a hazy apparition. The explanation that seems appropriate now is that I detached. My shock and pain were so consuming that there was little else to my existence. The impact was so deep I simply can't remember what transpired. I want to. I think I should be able to conjure up every sordid, ugly detail of the aftermath of an event that may have scarred me for life. I remember lying in a pool of tears that matted my hair and swelled my eyes shut as I curled into a ball on the bathroom floor, listening to the sound of my wailing as it reverberated against the cold porcelain tile. I remember the mountain of snot-filled tissues that cradled my head. But try as I might, time and memory are marked more by what I didn't do. Although they're terrible analogies, the effect was not unlike childbirth or orgasm, where everything around you simply ceases to exist, temporarily shoved into some other dimension because your body and mind can only focus on the intensity of what is happening between your legs.

Then again, perhaps the analogy is fitting, considering the irony. We are talking about infidelity after all.

I didn't fly back to Chicago, load his possessions into his car, and light it on fire à la Angela Bassett in *Waiting to Exhale*. I didn't call everyone we knew and vomit out sordid, hate-filled details of his betrayals. I didn't immediately hire the biggest, baddest SOB divorce attorney I could find to destroy him, delighting in the long list of people called for deposition just so my attorney could ask questions embarrassing enough to tarnish his professional reputation permanently.

I should have. Most women would have.

As time has passed, I've endlessly wrestled with my inaction in uncomfortable, self-loathing ways. *Why didn't I?* Castrating him with a rusty pocketknife would have been appropriate. The best explanation I've been able to formulate is twofold. I was too traumatized to think, let alone act. Nothing was safe. And deep under the surface, I knew none of it was about me.

Which was also the problem. None of it was about me.

So I existed, simply a ball of empty flesh alone on the bathroom floor, barely able to dress most days, unable to process, shutting it all down. I racked my brain with the unanswerable question, how does a man who had shown me so much love have it in him to live such a horrifying secret life without concern for his wife's welfare, let alone her love?

Initially, when he returned from rehab, we blundered through life in this place of unimaginable mutual pain. My husband, having just completed inpatient treatment, moved to outpatient, attended AA, and promised his therapy would continue. He promised he would get help figuring out the connections between the drinking and his adultery, because of course they were related. He promised we would go to therapy together.

He promised he would never, ever, ever, ever hurt me again.

I was too destroyed to do anything other than force myself to breathe.

What memories I do have of that period are few and painful and lack a cohesive timeline, yet they puncture my brain like shards.

My throat clenching and body trembling as I sat on an exam table in a paper gown waiting to be tested for STDs.

Waking up on the floor moments after passing out from stress, my blood pressure plummeting, taking me down. Then days later, gripping the steering wheel of my car in a panic as the blackness began to close in on me a second time.

Silently repeating to myself every night, "I will not let him destroy me! I will not let him destroy me!" as I stared at the ceiling, tortured by the images, real and imagined, that spiraled in my brain.

Feeling I'd never be happy again.

The crushing emptiness.

His behavior was now forced into the light of day, and having just left treatment where openness is considered essential, we attempted to have a conversation about his ugliness. Sitting in our living room one night like strangers who knew each other's most intimate secrets, he said, "I know it doesn't seem like it, but I love you. I've always loved you. I never took my ring off."

"Is that intended to make me feel better?" I said, the bile of disgust in my throat. "You didn't lie to these women about being married. You only lied to *me* about being married."

He looked confused, as if he were grasping for words, and stared at our dog, Bailey, sleeping at his feet.

"It was just sex," he mumbled, still not looking at me.

"Would it have been 'just sex' if I had done it?" Silence. "Is that what you want? A don't-ask-don't-tell marriage? You don't get to live by a separate set of standards and be married to me."

"No, that's not what I want." His voice was barely a whisper as he imagined what my retaliation might look like.

I had the sense that he thought displaying emotional distance from his physical acts would somehow smooth the rough edges of his behavior. Maybe it made him feel like less of a horrible shit, or maybe he thought he would soften me up with some pathetic "you're the only one I love, so please don't leave me" sentiment.

Or maybe he still hadn't shed his compartmentalized "both things can be true" thinking—a concept he had not yet processed for its utter hypocrisy.

Having lived with a booze-infected brain and a lie always at the ready, facing someone else's reality or pain now that he was sober seemed difficult for him, but it only left anger's bitter taste in my mouth.

The apologies and promises rained on me even when I was too distraught to hear them.

"I'll never hurt you again."

"I won't ever drink again."

"I'll figure out why I've been such an asshole."

"We'll go to therapy together."

"I promise I'll spend the rest of my life proving that I deserve you."

"Please don't leave me."

We were in Florida then, having purchased a condo just before he went to rehab for our new snowbird, semiretired lifestyle, intending to split our time between Chicago and Naples as the weather dictated. We'd stare at the ocean from our beachfront balcony, take morning walks on the sand, and celebrate the luxury that hard work had afforded us. I had closed my business for this—sold off my equipment and inventory, let go of staff—knowing that I couldn't operate from two states, not if I wanted my husband to stay sober. But that was before I knew the truth. When I still believed booze was the only problem.

Now what? I'd upended my life for him, and this is what he delivered. But he was honoring his commitment to AA and meeting regularly with a therapist. I, on the other hand, remained a quivering, retching, gutted mess. I knew I needed to leave. That there couldn't possibly be a scenario where I would get past his reprehensible behavior. But emotionally, I remained tethered to the love I still felt for him, the love I believed he had felt for me, and I couldn't make myself leave. My head and my heart were looping through the horrific disconnect between the love that felt deep and real and the hidden behavior that was anything but. How was it possible to have felt such love from a man, for a man, who could do this to us? It froze me, like a computer stuck in a reboot that would not end.

It suppose it was my own compartmentalization.

So I sought out a therapist. Yes, a new one. The "I usually work with the drunk" wasn't going to be what I needed for this either.

I walked into her dark little room in an office park one evening. An aromatherapy diffuser sat on a table releasing the scent of Palo Santo.

A salt lamp glowed in a corner, and a tall bookcase jammed with jargony self-help tomes lined the wall.

I sat in a well-worn chair and haltingly downloaded the CliffsNotes version of my marital problems.

"Would you like medication?" she promptly asked.

Being numb was supposed to help me sort out why I hadn't yet run as far away from this man as I could get?

"I'd prefer not to," I said quietly. I had no experience with antidepressants but imagined it as a quick-fix, medication-induced minor zombie state that would only delay the inevitable progression through my emotions until I could face them. Like it or not, I needed to feel this hurt. My decline wasn't an ethical issue, I simply didn't see how numbing my heart would fix anything.

In the next session—my chest still tight, my heart still destroyed, feeling so lost it was as if the world would never, ever look the same again—she suggested journaling as a methodology for dealing with the grief that was consuming me, the grief that had me lost at the bottom of a dark pit with no light and no ladder. Her suggestion horrified me.

I wasn't sure what terrified me more: the idea that my most intimate thoughts and fears would be memorialized in print where they could be discovered, read, and my vulnerability laid bare, or if it was the act of committing those thoughts to paper that was my true fear. Committing thoughts to paper would make them real. There would be no hiding from the anguish, the reality of my husband's behavior. The sheer ugliness could not be something I consolidated into a sound bite if I wrote it down. The fear was the realization that each individual ugly thought and feeling of anger and pain and betrayal would be all bundled up into one huge overwhelming thing.

To write it down, to write down every word that had been said, every moment of pain, every bit of ugliness would have broken me into a million pieces, particularly if it was read by others—those pieces would then need to be dealt with. I would have had to face the entirety of the problem, not the consolidated version that had become my mental elevator pitch because it seemed small enough to manage. It was the enormity of seeing it all that I could not face, I suspect.

I imagine the horror I felt was as obvious as an angry, infected gash on my face. I replied, "I couldn't do that. My husband would find it." We didn't discuss it much at the time. In hindsight, I wonder why. I knew what the emotion was; I knew it made my chest so tight that my breathing was strained. I couldn't bear the mere thought of my husband or anyone else discovering the journal and therefore leaving me even more exposed. It would have been a blow to the wound that would have crushed me into fragments at a time when the threads that held me together were gossamer thin.

Now, years later, it's clear she should have pushed me. I should have pushed myself to understand where that fear really came from, to understand why the risk of exposure terrified me so. But the conversation ended with my refusal, and it didn't come up again for weeks.

Not long after, she started the march down the "honey, get thee to a divorce lawyer pronto" path. She didn't see that although I knew intellectually divorce was the proper path, my heart was feeling rushed and forced and fearful. She wasn't wrong—even through the pain, I knew that much—but she also wasn't seeing me where I was. Somehow, the deep, fearful vulnerability I felt then wasn't clear to her, or perhaps she interpreted my lack of total collapse as stoicism.

I didn't feel stoic. I felt trapped by the pain, frozen, unable to move, to think, to act. Despite outward appearances, I was a trembling mess, barely able to breathe. I was still in shock and stayed there for months.

I'm not sure why, but I hid my initial therapist visits from my husband, only telling him after the session when I was processing the less than subtle "divorce his sorry ass ASAP" message. Did I expect him to have a negative reaction? Or did I just not think it was important for him to know?

Returning home after a session, I fessed up when he gave me a quizzical look as I walked into the kitchen.

"I was at a therapy appointment. I've been seeing her for three weeks."

He stared at me, his hand unmoving on the bottle of water he'd been opening.

"Why didn't you wait? I told you I'd arrange couples therapy," he said, then stalked off to sulk.

I followed him into his office. "Nothing is stopping you from making an appointment for the two of us. And in the meantime, *I* need help."

Was he avoiding making the appointment? Was his reaction to my treatment out of fear because he couldn't control the outcome? After all, if I talked to someone objective, someone outside our bubble, who in their right mind would say, "Sure. Stay with *this* guy. *That* will end well."

Two weeks later, I packed a bag and drove north to St. Petersburg, Florida, for a writing conference I had long since reserved. I thought it would feel good to get away from him and stay in a hotel and focus my thoughts on my novel. Maybe without the minute-by-minute reminders of his betrayal every time I saw his face, I could distract myself enough to finish the draft, could get closer to knowing how I wanted to move forward in my marriage. But the pain packed its own suitcase, becoming a stow-away in the moments I was alone in my room, the moments I was alone for dinner, in the moments between workshop sessions.

It would not leave me. Instead, my aloneness magnified my hurt.

I couldn't hold it in anymore, and there was no place to release my rage. So one day during lunch break, I left my fellow writers and sat alone in my car and stared at my phone, my body racked with grief, sobbing uncontrollably. Somehow, my car was the only place it felt safe to hear my own voice. The only place no one could witness or interrupt my breakdown. I swallowed gulps of air between each sob and made an appointment to consult with a divorce lawyer.

My novel had been only marginally advanced when I returned to Naples after the conference. I sat with my attorney discussing fees and legal process, giving the briefest of answers to the reason I was contemplating divorce and an overview of our assets. Then I asked the big question, "How ugly is this going to be?"

"We can't know that yet," she said diplomatically. "We'll have some idea based on his choice of counsel. But you need to be prepared for him to fight. There is a lot on the line. And I strongly advise you to make sure you have liquid assets he can't touch before you proceed. All of your accounts are jointly held. He could drain your cash. We'd get that money back, but it could take three months."

"So that's a tactic men use to control their wives? She'll acquiesce if she can't pay her attorney or feed herself?"

"That's the intent, yes. And hiding assets is common, so get copies of every financial document you can; that way if assets are moved, we have a record. And judges are not fond of that game."

She was telling me this would be a money fight. I imagined most divorces were, at least on the surface. Or the process itself turned the conflict into a fight for money. But that wasn't my fear. Fear of my financial situation on the other side wasn't keeping me in my marriage, and I knew that was a luxury many women didn't have. My children were out of the house by then, so custody and child support were not issues. I would not be destitute. My fears of the divorce process were about the emotional toll. I was barely functioning. How would I find my backbone for a scorched-earth divorce? It would send me back to that place on the bathroom floor.

I was still frozen with shock. It seems strange to think back on that now, to try to understand my emotional state and the way I remained locked in place. Time and healing layer in logic. But I simply couldn't act. My mind wouldn't let me, even when whispers of "I needed to leave" ran up the side of my neck.

Would staying have consequences too?

My mind looped our past with my now. The future was a black hole in my universe too vast to explore. I'd known women forced to stay in bad relationships, in places of hurt layered with love, because of the economics or the fear or because of children. A place where emptiness becomes the new normal, and you'd better be damn grateful for that. Right?

Isn't that the bargain women are expected to make? "Keep the family together. Love conquers all. The children need you. He really does love you underneath it all." Aren't those the words we hear? They're messages we are sent again and again and again by well-meaning friends, family, our community, our religions, our society. Our wants and needs and hurts as women are secondary because . . . family. Live with it, dammit, and be grateful for what you have. After all, you've got a pretty good life.

One evening, my husband convinced me to go out for dinner, suggesting a night out that felt normal would be good for us. I agreed, not because I thought the diversion would help our marriage but because I just didn't want to be alone with him anymore.

He made a reservation at one of the hot spots on Fifth Avenue South. Open-air cafés lined the sidewalks, tourists and seasonal residents strolled, and "see and be seen" was the motto "in season." It was a Friday night, a day of the week when we normally avoided that part of town, preferring quieter environments.

Seated near the wide-open patio doors, we managed banal conversation about the quality of the fish and commented about our ability to dine alfresco in February as if we were visiting business acquaintances in town for a weekend jaunt. An associate from one of my husband's corporate boards spotted us and stopped by to say hello, making meaningless chitchat about an upcoming meeting and a new restaurant he thought we needed to try. I made it through the meal without outbursts or tears, but everything about the evening grated on me. The noise. The crowd. The frivolity of those around us while I was masking my hurt, wrapping it up in a false skin—a costume.

The evening had been a mistake. As I drove us home, anger swelled inside me again like acid leaking onto my raw flesh.

"I have to run into New York the end of next week for a meeting," he said as we drove.

"What's her name? Is this someone new or one of your former lovers?" I snapped.

"I'm not seeing someone," he said, trying to keep his tone low, moderated, to hold me back from the brewing storm he sensed coming. "I'm interviewing a new board candidate. It's only one night."

But I was beyond the influence of a calm voice. "Sure!"

The barbs kept coming. I threw them at him for ten, maybe fifteen minutes, escalating into a typhoon of hurt.

By the time we stepped off the elevator and into our condo, we were both sparking with anger.

"You've had a pretty good life!" he shot at me as we walked into the foyer.

These were words uttered to remind me of my place in the hierarchy. Right. He gave me a nice house, so apparently, he was entitled to a little extracurricular sex. *Oh, okay, thank you, honey. I'll just go admire my beautiful kitchen and ignore your repeated betrayals as if my shredded heart or mind or soul doesn't mean anything at all. Thank you for explaining it to me so clearly. And go to hell!*

I was dismissed as irrelevant in six simple words.

I spat out, "Fine! I'll leave after Lisa is gone!" as a friend was arriving the next day for a short vacation. Then I left him standing in the foyer.

But I couldn't let that be the end. I changed my clothes and joined my husband in the living room, sat down on the opposite end of the couch, and screamed all the hurtful, ugly things I hadn't yet said. He got quiet, responding with something inane and patronizing about the neighbors hearing me through the open terrace door. I simply screamed louder while scanning the coffee table for something sharp and dangerous to throw at his head. His eyes got wide, and he looked at me like he'd never seen me before, like he didn't know who I was at that moment.

He looked scared. I *was* scared. I'd never felt myself this way. Had never felt such uncontrolled rage. I didn't know I was capable of the urge to inflict bodily harm, and I didn't know how close I was to doing something about it.

Why had I been controlling my pain and anger? More "good-girl" behavior? "Good girls" don't scream. They don't rail against those who've hurt them. More of the stay small, keep quiet, and behave shit that controls women's behavior. Men can rage. Women need to suffer silently, letting their hearts turn rancid with decay.

I didn't leave that night either.

Our calendar had been filled long before reality forced itself on me, and our new Florida guest room had been reserved for weeks out by friends and family anxious to escape the midwestern winters.

That next day, my friend Lisa flew in from Illinois. She'd made plans to visit for several days, and I couldn't ask her to cancel her trip on such short notice, and when she arrived, I didn't tell her. I hugged her at the airport, confession on the tip of my tongue. I sat with her on our terrace as my painful truth burned silently in my throat. I couldn't bring myself to share my pain. We only saw each other once every year or two; I didn't want to disrupt her vacation with my sad, pathetic turn of events. And I didn't want to face the embarrassment of what had been happening, so I put on the mask, placid that it was. Everything was fine. I existed drained of life, mechanically moving through the day, reminding myself I was supposed to smile. To laugh when I was expected to laugh. Autopilot to the rescue, again.

In hindsight, it was just another pointless "good-girl" move. Why was I embarrassed? I can't explain that. If she noticed the flat look on my face or heard the joy drained from my voice or sensed that life had gone out of me, she didn't let on. I was too wrapped up in holding my grief close to notice.

Or, perhaps, I was too well practiced in my silence.

We spent our days sitting under an umbrella on the beach or at the pool, talking about old friends and books, catching up on life. And each night I'd crawl into bed with my husband and sob.

"I don't want to be like that," I said, referencing my friend. "I don't want this anger to be a shield the way hers is." I cried into his chest as he wrapped his arms around me and pulled me close, into that spot where my head fit perfectly against his shoulder. The place I thought had been mine alone. And at that moment, I let him. He knew what I meant. He had been my source of solace for two decades. There had been nothing more consistently comforting than to be pressed against his chest. And I was desperate for a moment, however brief, to feel my world would be safe again.

"You won't. We're going to be okay," he said. "I promise. I'll never hurt you again."

This friend had divorced years earlier, after her husband left her for someone else, and she still wore her hurt. It frightened me the way she had hung on to her pain for so long, seemingly allowing it to drain her of joy and hold her back from a full life.

Would this man I had adored leave me bitter, forever unable to trust, robbing me of even more than what I thought had been our marriage?

Days after my friend left, the next round of guests arrived—my parents. They had been divorced for many years but remained friends.

The first few days were easy, at least as far as the mess of my marriage was concerned. My mother had just been diagnosed with pancreatic cancer and our attention was on her. The trip south had been my treat, a distraction before she began her treatment. A vacation she wouldn't have given herself. We weren't particularly close, but none of that mattered anymore. I had long since set aside lingering expectations of what "mom" was supposed to be. She lived by her own rules. She dealt out empathy and compassion with a joke or a laugh or a long look, not a hug.

We, too, sat by the pool, enjoying the luxury of having cocktails delivered to our lounge chairs late in the afternoon as if being catered to at a resort, and marveling at the pelicans and dolphins playing in the surf. Every night, we continued our new beach-life custom and walked down to watch the sunset, then dined on the terrace as the sky faded from pinks and oranges to black, listening to the crash of the surf.

My husband left for his New York business trip, and my mother flew back to Wisconsin a few hours later to start her cancer treatment.

Early that evening, I sat alone on the terrace trying to read, enjoying the quiet. My father stepped out, standing in front of me with his old-fashioned in hand.

"Why are you so sad?" he said, looking down at me.

I set aside my book, trying to swallow tears that were bubbling to the surface. I debated what to say, how much to tell him. The enormity of my pain pressed down on my heart.

"My husband is an alcoholic," I said. "We've been battling it for years. He just spent six weeks in rehab. And while he was there, I learned he's had affairs."

I couldn't say more. Couldn't get out the words that would have added any context to the situation. But I didn't need to, not for him. My father is not a man of deep, heartfelt conversation. "Just the facts, ma'am," was enough.

He responded with his characteristic "Hmmph." The length of which serves as an indicator of emotion.

"You never know what happens in another man's house." This was his only additional comment. He had no questions. No "I'm so sorry." No "Can I do anything for you?"

Conflict rumbled in me. Anxiety released its grip; the brevity of his response required no regurgitation of details of what or when or why. Or even an admission that I myself didn't know. Yet there was no strong shoulder of support either. His moral support would need to be assumed rather than shown.

Lacking another response, I stood. "I'm going to get a glass of wine." But what I really wanted was to get away from the emotional void that had widened in front of me. And as I walked into the kitchen I thought, *Thanks for the misogyny, Dad.*

———————

"Is love enough?"

I sat silently, contemplating the therapist's question, unable to answer. She'd asked me why I was still there. Why I had not yet left him. And I'd replied with what seemed the most obvious of answers.

"I still love him. Not his behavior, of course, but him."

I had not separated the man I thought I knew from the version of him who was capable of treating me with disrespect and committing reprehensible acts of betrayal.

Feeling ripped open and forlorn in my chair in her dark, tiny, depressing office where the walls closed in until I wanted to run, I said nothing more in response that day. I had no answer. Part of me understood what she wanted me to see—there is no love without trust and respect. And through his behavior, my husband had shown himself eminently unworthy of mine. But I also remained locked in the very real demonstrations of love I'd experienced in our life together and in my memories and in the knowledge that he was doing the hard work of getting sober, for me. Doing it first because he loved me and wanted me to remain in his life, then because he wanted to love himself.

Sitting in her office, I was too deep in the raw, bloody emotion of betrayal to discuss analytically the difference between my intellectual truths and my emotional truths, but her question pierced through the pain and stuck with me even though I chose to set it aside to deal with later.

"Here, I think this would be helpful." She pulled a book off the shelf behind her and handed it to me. "You can pick up a copy on Amazon."

The Wizard of Oz and Other Narcissists.

Two weeks later, I'd digested the book and had an additional conversation with my therapist. The author's description of narcissism had made me feel better in a weird way. A diagnosis was something tangible, I guess, a medical condition, something that went beyond "He's just a selfish jackass trying to hurt me."

"My therapist and I have been discussing narcissism," I said to my husband one night. His jaw clenched and I could see the irritation in his eyes. He didn't need me to explain we were applying the diagnosis to him.

"What do *you* think?" he asked.

"I think it's one possible explanation for your selfish behavior."

He walked out of the room. Three days later, he brought up the subject himself. "Dr. Stewart says you can exhibit narcissistic behaviors without *being* a narcissist."

Ah yes, the suggested diagnosis had offended him, and he'd run straight to his shrink to disprove my therapist's theory. It felt like proof of something to me, even if I was the only one who saw the distinction as splitting hairs.

In my attempt to understand the unfathomable, I grasped at straws that made sense to me—books. I picked up a copy of *After the Affair*, hoping, I suppose, someone could explain it to me in a way that could mitigate my hurt. Explain why any of this had happened. Tell me what I should do now to fix me. The book was intended as a guide for coming to terms with the grief of infidelity and how to find a way through. The author wrote that men often say the affair was "just sex" and that the woman betrayed should believe them. It probably was nothing more to them. This was given as an explanation, I assumed, to understand the compartmentalization that men are capable of when they want to get laid. A way for women to feel less personally destroyed.

What are men? Randy, indiscriminate dogs who are to be excused for humping the closest leg?

I'd heard those words myself. "It was just sex."

The empty hole inside of him that had brought this down on us was now an empty hole inside of me the size of a galaxy. The pain left me shredded and sick and questioning every moment of perceived love, every word he'd ever spoken to me, but I was to dismiss it because men put their hearts in a box they keep on a shelf when their dick needs attention. No, let me correct that, when their dick needs attention from someone new that they then hide from their partner. It was really about the rush of the secret, wasn't it? The conquest?

My husband's tone when he'd said those words to me told me he expected this explanation to ease my grief. As if "it meant nothing to *me*" wouldn't equate to "*you* meant nothing to me." She said it first. She did it first. The language of the cheat grasping at cobwebs for life support.

The hypocrisy was the hardest to stomach. The knowledge that his warped rationalizations wouldn't apply if the tables were reversed. I had been subjected to grilling and snooping and repeated bouts of jealousy and insecurity. There wasn't a question in my mind about the depth of the wrath I would have felt from him if I had dared to be the one who strayed. One moment of weakness or poor decision or drunken slip would have led him straight to a divorce attorney, no questions asked, regardless of his own secrets. Secrets he would have protected, hypocrisy be damned. And secrets on one side of the equation were intolerable.

Do cheaters ever understand the way razor blades slice into your heart at the briefest of reminders? Or is this only a female response? I don't have a focus group to poll on that issue, but I've wondered how the Mars crew reacts to these things when they're the ones who've been betrayed. We on the Venus side, we feel every slice.

On multiple occasions after learning of his infidelity, I smugly, angrily, reminded my husband that he had given me permission to entertain any dalliances *I* so chose. If that elicited jealousy and fear in him, it was his damn problem.

One spring evening, he was traveling, off to another board meeting in New York, and my insecurity was again smoldering. Thoughts of his hypocrisy swept me away. I stood in front of my lingerie drawer, lifted out a set of never-worn black lace La Perla bra and panties, and laid them on the bench. Then I opened the closet and pulled out a dress, tags still attached. Its soft silk caressed my hips; its neckline framed my collarbone and hinted at my curves. Stilettos. The smallest dap of perfume strategically placed. All purchased specifically for an evening like this, as were the condoms tucked inside a pocket of my small handbag. This was an evening I had known would come. I had felt the ugly, fearful jolt of guilty secrets when I bought my ensemble, but I purchased them anyway, feeling indignant and entitled and angry.

I placed my wedding ring in a drawer and drove down the beach to the Ritz-Carlton. Sliding onto a seat at the bar, I ordered a pricey cabernet and sipped it slowly as I admired the precision of the bottle display behind the bar. It wasn't long before a man took the empty stool next to me. I sipped my wine, tried to flirt, tried to make myself want to do what I clearly had come to do. He was attractive, charming, willing, and had a room at the hotel, but nothing about the exchange was sexy or fun. I did not desire this man. I did not desire this act. Instead, the cold void in me grew.

As I watched this stranger's gaze boldly linger on my breasts as I tried on the role of temptress, I heard my husband's voice play in my head: "It was just sex."

"Revenge sex," I heard in my own.

I finished my drink, declined the offer to join him upstairs that followed, and got the hell out of there. I showered off my failed attempt at adultery when I got home and cried myself to sleep, again.

I am not him.

I wanted to, I told myself, reasoning it was the right thing to do. I was entitled, believing I would feel more in control if I tipped the scales just the smallest amount, but my want was about power. My want was to hurt him back, not a desire for a quickie with a man I didn't know, or anyone else for that matter. Nonetheless, whether I did or didn't, the choice was mine and mine alone. That knowledge mattered to me. And it mattered that my husband knew it.

It was for me alone to decide if and who and why I shared my body. Even if I never did.

Not long after that night, my husband finally arranged couples therapy. It had been his commitment, so I hadn't inserted myself into the process, but I certainly noted how long it had taken for him to set it up. Our first two meetings were strained but yielded no revelations or answers. We each sat in her office, devastated, reliving the injury, regurgitating our individual versions of what had happened and how we felt.

I could hear the flatness in my own voice, as if I was reciting from a printed script outlining his failings. And my own. He did this, then I did that, and here we are. Every now and then, a sharp pang would sneak through as I spoke, like the pins and needles of a foot that had fallen asleep, reminding me of life outside of grief. But mostly our first sessions were simply a reminder of the empty void that had been my heart.

On the eve of our third appointment, I wandered through our home with dread, knowing there was a question I had to ask my husband. Something that had been lurking under the surface for me that I hadn't explored in the pain of "why?" And I expected his answer would likely be the last thread to break.

"How was your week? Is there anything that came up that either of you wants to talk about?" the therapist asked us.

"I have something. Something that I felt I needed to discuss here," I said quickly, afraid that if I didn't start, I might not get the words out.

"That's good. Go ahead," she said, nodding.

I clutched my thighs to hide my shaking, then turned to my husband. "I've brought up the fact that I've gone in for STD testing on three occasions. But not once have you asked a single question about that. Why?"

Startled, as any woman would be, the therapist jumped in before he could respond. "I assumed you had dealt with that already."

I kept my eyes on my husband as he stared at the floor, his elbows on his knees, refusing to look at me. "Well, you're still sleeping with me so there can't be a problem," he said. Indignation rippled in his voice.

My mouth dropped open with rage, and my hands curled into fists.

"This is my life!" I said. "What if I'd contracted HIV?" I was disgusted with his response, with him, I shook my head and stared at the floor myself. I hadn't pegged his exact words, but the callous "why would I care about that?" sentiment was exactly what I had feared and, sadly, expected. The subject would have forced him to unbox his past, would have forced him to break down the compartmentalization he desperately wanted to remain intact. I could easily imagine him saying, "But, I'm a good guy now. Can't we stick with that?"

The gut punch left me breathless yet again.

"This is pointless," I said, wanting to go back to that place on the bathroom floor. Then after a pause that felt interminable, where my body churned with anger and disappointment and resignation, I blurted out, "You self-centered prick!"

Calmly, I picked up my bag and walked out of the therapist's office using every ounce of self-control I had and numbly wandered through the parking lot, then toward home. Ten minutes later, I was on the phone with my divorce lawyer.

CHAPTER NINE
DIVORCE NUMBER ONE

The ten-ton weight on my chest again pinned me to the floor, and my red-rimmed eyes were swollen shut with tears. My husband moved into the guest room but remained in the apartment, torturing me with his presence. I cloistered myself in our bedroom so I wouldn't have to see him. Wouldn't have to decide minute by minute whether to hate him for breaking my heart or to hate myself for breaking his when I saw the pain in his eyes.

After a week of agony, I marched into his office and insisted he leave. He grudgingly packed up and returned to Chicago with our dog. And the sound of my sobbing filled the empty rooms again.

Hurt beyond hurt, I couldn't write. I couldn't think. I couldn't eat. Instead, I spent weeks tracing other people's footsteps on the beach, oblivious to the beauty of the Gulf, walking until I looked up and didn't recognize where I was. In our apartment, I'd scan the beautiful rooms thinking I should sit on the living room sofa, read, even turn on the fireplace on a chilly night, but thoughts of such normalcy repulsed me. This was no longer a home; it was a mausoleum. The apartment now served as a constant reminder of what our life was supposed to have been. I could only see that the life we thought we were starting here was nothing but a hand trick, an illusion, just like our marriage had been.

It was September by then, and most mornings, I forced myself to go to the nearest Barnes & Noble. I would pack my laptop and my notebook and park myself at a table with a cup of tea and stare at my screen trying not to cry. I'd nurse the hot drink until it was cold and tasteless, eventually finding an excuse to roam the aisles when the words didn't come that day either.

Every once and awhile, some stupid schmuck would notice my bare ring finger and try to engage me in banter or come straight out and suggest a dinner date, and since this was Naples, some version of "Can I tell you how rich I am?" would be part of the pitch. I'd recoil and give him a look that suggested he had oozing open sores on his face and bury my head back in the blank screen in front of me. The thought of small talk with a guy, let alone one who led with "Date me because I have money," induced thoughts even more vile than the ones running through my mind inside the empty cage that was my home.

Eventually, the business of divorce pulled me out of the bookstore, keeping me in the apartment downloading, copying, and gathering documents.

One morning, I walked barefoot into the spare bedroom I was using as an office, a steamy cup of Earl Grey in hand, my head foggy from another sleepless night, my cat sprawled on the folders I had left in neat piles on the floor the day before as I organized the mountains of financial documents. Sitting down at my desk, I opened an email to find a note from the paralegal at my attorney's office. It simply said, "See attached correspondence from opposing counsel."

It was a request for documents. As I ran through the request, spasms formed deep in my stomach.

He wanted journals. He wanted private investigator reports. He wanted taped phone calls. He wanted to know how much I knew and how much I could prove of my husband's infidelities.

They wanted to know what dirt I had that was provable in court, and they were going to use that to negotiate against me. After all, if I didn't have video, had it happened?

Regardless of what my husband had admitted to, this seemingly simple request was an attorney throwing down the gauntlet, letting me know that the fight was about to get ugly.

Scorched-earth ugly.

Isn't that how the legal process works?

I shook with vulnerability and horror. They wanted me to expose the raw, naked emotion, the destruction of my heart and my soul to a group of male strangers, who I assumed underneath it all were probably of the "good for him" mindset. The ugly, notches on the belt, "don't we all wish we were a stud" mindset. I didn't know these guys, I didn't know this attorney, but why would my husband choose anyone who wasn't able to sympathize with him in some way or envy his conquests or place blame on me for not being able to meet his needs? After all, isn't that how men think? "Go for it if you can. He must not be getting any at home."

He hadn't chosen a female attorney, that was clear. He went for the bulldog who I assumed had no qualms about destroying any last ounce of self-respect or dignity I might still possess. My hands shook as I printed off the document and read the request a second time, then out of reflex, my legs returned to pacing the room, forcing breath into my lungs.

I phoned my attorney, panic punctuating each word I spoke, but she was out of the office and the paralegal had no additional advice. So I hung up, called my therapist, and tried to move up my appointment, but she, too, had other commitments.

For nearly a full day, I mindlessly roamed from room to room, unable to control my emotions, not sure what to do with myself. I raged at the walls, pain and anger competing for attention. Anger won out. And over a period of four days, I sat down and gave them what they wanted. I bought myself a lovely notebook chosen specifically to have the right tone—nothing too sweet or girlie, this was war—then sat alone in an apartment I now despised for what it represented, and I wrote and I cried and I flailed at the empty pages, at the walls that should have been full of love. I re-created every moment, every word said, every painful image and emotion that I had been carrying with me, released every painful, disgusting thought in my head, and I committed it all to paper.

I thought, *Okay, you want to know what this is like? I. Will. Show. You.* Part of me never expected that my husband would be able to face the pain evident on those pages. He wouldn't read it, but his attorney would. And if he wanted to know how I felt, what had been said between a husband, a wife, and occasionally, a therapist, I was going to show him. Every ugly, disgusting moment of my agony would be there on the page for them to see.

I would be heard.

Days later, at my next therapist appointment, I told her what I had done. I can still remember the tone in my voice. An almost triumphant "Fuck you!" directed at my husband. She asked how long it had taken me to re-create the events from memory, but there were no additional questions about what or why or how that felt. At the time, it didn't seem relevant, and I didn't wonder about it. Perhaps I was still too consumed with anger. Perhaps I simply couldn't process any additional emotions.

I've thought about that journal many times over the last few years. A journal that is still safely tucked away, locked in a safe-deposit box. A journal that holds my true self.

An insurance policy.

After another morning tapping the keyboard at the Starbucks inside Barnes & Noble, I got a few hundred bland, boring, unusable words onto the page. My mind simply could not stop playing movies of my history or movies of how I imagined my husband lived, dwelling on the falseness of it all, and I was struggling to make progress with my draft. Around twelve thirty, I packed my things and walked over to one of the nearby restaurants for a lunch break. I had just been seated when my phone rang.

It was my father.

"Your mother died this morning. Jackie found her on her couch."

"I'll be on the next plane."

Her funeral was brief and no frills, just like her. It was held in a room without fanfare, adorned only with the standard bouquets of death—carnations, lilies, baby's breath—and a formal photo of her taken years before at some company required headshot session when she'd been a bookkeeper. Longtime friends, from her decades in the tiny northern Wisconsin community and her years of tending bar, showed up in their flannel and their sweatshirts. They told stories of Bonnie's jokes and feisty temperament and "remember the time she . . ." And I saw they were full of love for this woman who rarely put up with shit even when common sense should have advised her to hold her tongue.

If we'd thought about it, setting up a bar right there in the back of Gaffney's Funeral Home would have made her smile. None of us were surprised by the outcome, just the speed at which pancreatic cancer claimed her. She smoked and drank and hit the casino right until the end. Not even life-threatening cancer would change her. Her lifestyle wasn't mine, and I had conflicting feelings about the version of "mom" she had shown us, but I admired her ability to live her life with pride.

After the ceremony and burial and required post-service buffet, my siblings and I sat around her kitchen table combing through her recipe box, pulling out our favorites to create a family cookbook. "She made the best chili." "I've never been able to get her butterballs exactly right." "I always make Hello Dolly bars for the night we decorate the Christmas tree." The memories of food were deeply intertwined with our childhoods, and each of us grappled with our confused feelings of loss and love and what we felt for our mother.

We cleared out her fridge and her closets and bathroom. Holding on to personal treasures. Looking for cash she'd told us she'd hidden in the apartment after her latest casino win. Telling stories, mostly about times she had embarrassed us as children. I stayed for a week, spending time with my dad and doing what I could to clean up the small apartment building she owned, as it would be sold.

That evening after the family was gone, I sent my husband a text letting him know she had died. I waited for my phone to ring. It didn't.

But I spent the next day desperate to hear his voice, looking anxiously at my phone for a missed text or a missed call. I wanted nothing more than for him to hold me. As hurt as I was by his behavior, all I wanted, still in my confused grief, was to feel his arms around me.

About twenty-four hours later, the text came. Dad and I were visiting a family friend for dinner, and he sent me a note telling me how sorry he was about my mother. I couldn't help myself and sent back, "I wished that you had called."

Not two seconds later, my phone rang. I stepped outside to answer.

"I didn't think you'd want to hear from me," my husband said haltingly. "I'm sure you hate me. And I didn't want to add any more pain."

"I don't hate you," I said, not bothering to choke back the tears. "I'm hurt and angry, and I don't understand. But she was your mother-in-law, and I thought you should have been able to set aside our stuff to at least offer me your condolences."

So again we cried together over my mother, over all of our hurt, over all of our love needlessly trampled on and discarded. Love and hate. Anger and relief. Betrayal and adoration. I couldn't separate the emotions anymore. Once again, they buried me, pulling me into a place where I couldn't see what I wanted or know with certainty how I felt about him. The man I loved, the man I thought I had been married to, was present in that call, not the man who betrayed me. And it froze me once again.

And it also reopened a sliver of my heart.

I returned to Florida, confused about how I could still feel anything for a man who had gutted me with his blind selfishness. The only thing I knew for certain was that when we spoke, a piece of me felt whole again.

"Before you make a decision, talk to three friends. Ask them what they think about staying married to an alcoholic who has betrayed you repeatedly."

I nodded solemnly at my therapist and promptly tossed her suggestion in the trash.

She wasn't wrong, I knew that. The rethinking I was doing about the divorce didn't hold up to the harsh magnifying glass of scrutiny and logic. But I was back in that discordant place of knowing that I should not stay married while, emotionally, not being ready to leave.

Not ready to stop loving him.

I also wasn't ready, then, to say it all out loud. Not every ugly detail. The thought sent spasms of fear through my body. I would rather have stood naked in front of a crowd of a hundred people and given a speech than utter my full unvarnished truth.

This therapist also didn't know my friends. My friends would have looked at me with sadness and empathy and their own raw pain and said, "What does your heart want?" and, "Do what you believe is right for you," even if they doubted the odds of success. They aren't friends who would be horrified and judgmental about my decision, regardless of whether I stayed or left. They would never claim to be able to tell me how I should feel even when rightly appalled by his behavior.

Yet, I still could not say my truth to them.

Time and emotions again blurred. I had no structure to process the contradictory things I was feeling. What happened, in what order, blurred. How I felt, what I did, what he did, when he did it, I can't say with any accuracy. So I have no framework now to recount how we got from that moment to one where the world again began to have color.

What I do know is that as the truth of my false life settled in, it morphed through stages of anger; endless, excruciating, tearful conversations; accusations; ongoing therapy; separation; divorce proceedings; more therapy; stress-related health issues; and eventually—surprisingly, shockingly, inconceivably—into reconciliation.

The moment I opened my heart to that possibility is clear. I'd flown to Chicago to gather some of the documents we needed for our divorce. The two of us in the same apartment for the first time in months, we sat in our kitchen one October day, the sun sparkling against the water, and I saw utter destruction in his face. I felt my heart clench, although I couldn't say it—didn't want to acknowledge the love still inside me, not to him. I didn't think he deserved my love. More than a year had passed since his boozed-up brain had controlled him, and he seemed stunned at himself, as if "that man" and "this man" were different beings. He spoke of the intensive therapy that he had continued since we'd separated to try to shake out the why of it all.

I knew he didn't have to explore this ugliness. He could have convinced himself that with the booze gone, the work had been done. The rest of it, well, it wasn't relevant post-divorce. But he didn't. He looked in the mirror, finally clear-eyed, and did the most painful thing a human being can do. He looked inside himself. He hated what he saw, hated the pain he had caused, hated himself for it.

Without any expectation that our marriage could be saved, he was doing the work. He was doing it for me.

"I guess I hope that one day, maybe, you might allow me back into your life," he said.

And eventually, I did.

Love was still present. Broken, bent, raw, hurting, we chose what we believed to be the harder path. Fighting for love.

Did that decision represent the best of love or the worst of being a woman?

Did my love blind me? Did my inherent empathy blind me? My very femaleness? I didn't think about it that way, not then. I didn't possess the capacity for those thoughts, still racked as I was with the pain. That question required a distance and clear-headedness I'm still not sure I possess.

What I knew was that I still loved him.

What I felt was that he still loved me.

And what I saw was a man doing every possible thing he could to be someone deserving of my love.

I paused the divorce proceedings, and we fell into a new, cautious routine. Two people, different, forever changed, trying to figure out what life together looked like after the worst. It's tempting to use the word *rebuilding*, but there is no rebuilding after the foundation has been razed and the earth beneath you is toxic and unstable. We needed something new.

Slowly, new emotions found their way to the surface as the ice began to melt and the shock began to wane. Little by little, a smile came back, a laugh, but with it were also new issues of trust. New fears, new tears, but each and every time I exploded in insecurity, I was shown respect and consistency, and humility. The defensive, often arrogant posture my husband had routinely taken during heated conversations in the past was gone, and in its place, a man humbled and patient and accepting of his punishment, regardless of the harshness of the momentary venom I spewed.

As I inched toward resuming our marriage, we began testing out cohabitation again. Back in Chicago, I walked into my husband's office one afternoon.

"I need a postnup," I said. "And I want you to propose the terms. What are you willing to put on the line to prove your commitment to me? What are you willing to sacrifice if you ever drink or lie to me or cheat on me again?"

He swallowed hard, then nodded.

"These are the new ground rules if we do this. Show me how badly you want me in your life," I said.

And he did.

"Seventy/thirty in your favor," he said a few days later.

"Sixty/forty is fine. Write it up and sign it."

My aim wasn't the money. It was a test. I wanted to elicit a commitment. I was putting him in a box where he would be forced to take responsibility for the outcome if we were to go forward, and therefore, could not blame me or an attorney or a judge, if he ever chose to violate our marriage again.

But secrets are insidious, and my husband still kept his disease close even after he was sober. Believing healing included chasing his addiction out of the shadows, I insisted that he reveal his illness to our family. None of them knew, beyond my father whom I'd told myself. He agreed, and I sat with him as he spoke to our boys—now in college—and again while he spoke with his daughters.

His announcements were succinct statements of fact. "I have a problem with alcohol. I went to rehab. I'm going to AA. I'm better now. I wanted you to know."

It wasn't the level of detail or emotion that I would have chosen to underscore the depth of his problem or the heartache he'd caused, but it wasn't my story to tell. The value was in the reveal. Others would now know and might notice signs of a relapse if it occurred. They could help him, and me, with accountability. At least, that was what I hoped for.

By then his daughters had families of their own, and when he left the room, I cautioned them that it had been far worse than he'd let on and asked that they check in with him periodically on his progress. I also asked my husband to tell my father personally along with my husband's best friend who had also been oblivious. Their responses were concerned, confused silence, or "Can't you just stop drinking?" It was the naivete of the uninitiated.

Despite my requests, not one of these people—the closest of people—ever to my knowledge followed up and asked him, "How's your sobriety? Are you managing?" No one would ask the hard questions.

Periodically, my father would throw a "how's it going?" question into the conversation, but only with me. And if my answer took more than two sentences, he would cut me off or change the subject. Our boys, I'll forgive, considering their age and hence their maturity level at the time; my stepdaughters, well, perhaps they have their own issues with silence.

Regardless, what mattered to me was that he declared it. He said the words, "I am an alcoholic," not to some room of strangers in an AA meeting but to the people we loved. The people he worried would judge him.

Not long after, my sister Kris visited me in Chicago, grabbing a little break while on a business trip. My husband was out that night, and we sat talking in my apartment, refreshing our bond, a glass of wine in hand. She, of course, plunged into "How are *you* doing?"

After I downloaded my own condensed version of my emotional pendulum, she eyed me tentatively, and asked, "Was there more than one?" She was asking the big question—the adultery question. All I could do was swallow, forcing down the knot that had formed in my throat, and reply, "Yes," my voice gripped with pain and fear.

She recoiled, and her silence felt like a cavern between us. "I don't think I could do that," she said after excruciating seconds passed.

There was no more. Whatever she was thinking, whatever questions she had but could not ask, whatever judgment she was making about my decision to stay, she kept to herself.

I was relieved. Typically, we could and did talk about anything. But not this. I couldn't defend my decision to stay in the marriage, not to her, fearing my conflicted thoughts, I suppose, or knowing my argument did not stand up to scrutiny, I suppose.

Despite the commitment we'd made to repairing and healing our marriage, indecision clawed back at me periodically, brought on by some triggering comment or memory or just plain fear that I had made the wrong choice—fear that I didn't know how to live with the way my imagination could fabricate events or history. There was the occasional heartbreaking thought that my entire marriage had been a lie. And there was disgust with myself when I couldn't decipher whether my decision was one of weakness or strength.

And the most haunting question of all was, "If you loved me, how could you have disrespected me so completely?"

It was himself he didn't respect. I'm just collateral damage, remember?

My husband knew he didn't deserve the grace I had shown him. No matter what I threw at him, over and over, his actions were consistent attempts to show me he deserved a place in my life, now, regardless of my insecurities or my fears. He showed me that he was a better, new, and improved version of himself, no longer missing his internal compass. No longer controlled by booze. And my love would roar back until something drew me down back into pain and indecision.

The episodes would play out, often just in my mind, and at times, they were gone in a matter of hours. Others would last for days, and the public displays of my raw, confused emotions were impossible to ignore as I railed. One moment sent me packing and sleeping at a hotel for several days, crying endlessly until my eyes were nearly swollen shut, then scouring apartment listings for a place to move. Alone, away from him. Another time, I slept at my painting studio, torn in two by the unanswerable questions and the disgust I felt with him and with myself. It was an urge to run away from the pain. A hope that distance would allow me to think more clearly. And some days, it was the inability to look at him without thinking, *How could you!*

But my indecision was never caused by some new behavior or even a suspicion of behavior. It was spurred by my conflicted feelings about my choice to stay, even though he was doing everything imaginable to try to make it right. Everything imaginable to show me love.

But who stays with a man who has repeatedly betrayed her? What kind of woman did that make me? Just a fool allowing herself to be trampled on? A woman with no self-respect? Why, in that moment of truth, did I not scream or strike or cut off his balls in his sleep? He sure as hell deserved it.

But questions about why I stayed were about me, and I didn't have the skill or distance to answer those hard truths.

Indecision was the punishment I inflicted on myself.

CHAPTER TEN
LOVE OR HATE? I CAN'T DECIDE

I should hate him, I know.

I'd known since that day at the rehab center when I learned the truth. That moment when my world crashed, and I knew that nothing I had believed to be true really was. There had been moments where I wished I hated him. Feeling that hatred would be easier than the path we were on. I'd certainly felt rage, moments when utter contempt blinded me and I found myself staring too long at my copy of *Deadly Doses: A Writer's Guide to Poisons*, which was on the bookshelf in my office along with the typical macabre collection of tomes that constitute a mystery writer's research library.

Apparently, I'm not killer material.

Underneath the agony, underneath the accumulated scar tissue that hardened my heart, and in those rough moments of doubt, I forced myself to remember that his behavior had nothing to do with me.

Alcoholism had given me enough insight to understand that his infidelity was just another symptom of his emotional void. Another vice he used to numb and deflect and self-destruct.

So I hated myself instead.

Why can I not rage? Why can I not scream and throw things and lash out with the indignity I feel? Why did I grow up to be a person who believes she must keep it together even when it feels wrong to do so?

Why is silence the place I have always felt safe?

Knowing he wasn't intentionally being cruel and heartless never stopped the ongoing debate inside me about what I could live with, what baggage I could carry around and still function. Even as the questions played out in my head and in my heart, I knew that love was still there, changed and minimized, but it was love, nonetheless.

As my therapist had asked: Is love enough? We're taught that it's supposed to be. Love conquers all, right?

But there is a price to be paid when the scale is tipped too far, and that was also my weight to carry.

The "stay or go" debate raged sporadically in me for several years. It was never pervasive enough to change my decision, but I can no longer count the number of times I was certain I couldn't go on, that the burden was too great to bear. The fear simply festered under the surface, waiting for a small crack of vulnerability to reveal itself so it could ooze out again.

Over time, the frequency of those thoughts diminished, and they no longer gripped me. I no longer kept a suitcase ready or plotted a strategy for moving out. Time would heal me, I believed. Eventually, I would return to a place where the rich love I had felt was present, I thought. Although the depth of my love had not been restored, it was impossible not to admire and respect the work he was doing to try to prove to me that he was a man worthy of my love, worthy of the chance I was giving him. Attentive, self-aware, he was a man doing the work he promised me. So, on the surface, life returned to normal, such that it could: from how we structured our day to how we existed together without animosity, settling into our marital shorthand.

But a hole now existed in me. An ever-present intruder. I poured writing and painting into that space. A full calendar was the warm blanket of diversion. But it's an inadequate middle-of-the-night companion when the raw, naked wound that hasn't closed screams for attention.

If you'd have asked me before COVID where I believed I was on the continuum in my healing, I would have said something along the lines of, "I'm doing okay. He's doing everything he needs to. I have some rough moments here and there, but they pass." And although it sounds like a rote, bullshit answer as I put it on the page now, it was what I believed to be true.

Good enough was enough. Eventually, the pain would fade as new layers of consistency were built, as his commitment to staying sober continued, as his commitment to our marriage was confirmed. I believed I could live with his history as we were doing the hard work together. We had chosen that.

In December 2019, before any of us had any idea how a pandemic was about to change our lives, I had drinks with my friend Jen. She, too, had experienced infidelity in her marriage, but for them, there was no path forward. I hadn't told her about my husband's secret life, but I had shared some aspects of his alcoholism.

"Is it good enough?" she asked, as we sat with our wine in the dark booth.

She of course meant, "Are you getting enough out of the relationship? It's not filling every need, but is it filling enough to remain?" She asked in part because she was questioning some of these things herself after dating a man for a couple of years. He wasn't a grand love, but for now, he was enough. She knew there would be a point in the future when one of them would need more. Although she didn't say it exactly that way to me, that was the question I knew she was asking.

I thought for a moment, then answered, "Yes, it's enough." Although conscious of the hurt still raging in my heart and conscious of the truth I was holding back, I believed it. I had chosen to live with our history. I had knowingly chosen the compromise.

Because my husband had done so much and worked so hard, doing something truly difficult and, in some ways, awe-inspiring to keep me in his life, I believed the love I still had for him could leave me happy enough in my life. Individually and jointly, we had decided to pursue the more difficult path with the full knowledge that one of the consequences of our journey was that he loved me more and that I loved him less than before. It was a trade-off we knowingly made. It had been said out loud. *I* had said it out loud.

"I love you less."

"I hope you can learn to love me the same way again," he said with hurt in his eyes. It went unsaid that it would have to be enough for each of us.

Life moved on, falling into a pattern, as life does, and our fraught emotional conversations became less frequent; our days again became routine. We worked, we played, we loved, we made love, we planned for our future, we forged something new, something different from what we had before. Our relationship resembled the before time on the surface, but underneath, there was a new current. Through therapy, my husband had become a more attentive, empathetic partner. Over and over and over he showed me his commitment to being a better man, a better husband.

Slowly, and with fits and starts, I began to view my wound as no longer life-threatening, but as an injury that required physical therapy. Like a leg that had received multiple fractures, I would walk again, but there would be a change in my gait or a lingering throb when the night air was too cold. The scar would be there forever, and it was up to me to make choices about how to minimize its appearance in my life. I was determined not to let our history destroy me. I said it loud and often to myself, just as I had in the early days of my grief as I lay on the bathroom floor, ravaged with hurt: "This will not destroy me." Willing it to be true through the force of repetition. Somehow, I had to find the silicone scar strip for shattered hearts.

We had chosen the harder path, because love was worth fighting for.

And this was our life, this is where we were, little by little, trying to heal. It wasn't very rich or full of life or love. *I* wasn't as full of life or love, but I believed that time would heal us.

Then COVID hit.

———————

I stared out of the window of the plane at the mountains, smiling down with anticipation, taking in the rocky crags, watching the way the sun cast its light on the ridges, illuminating them until they glowed blissful shades of orange and pink and purple.

Four days of blissful girl time with my dear friend Ann were ahead of me. We were meeting in Tucson for the Gem Show, where I'd tag along while she shopped for stones and other findings for her jewelry line. I'd vicariously play designer as she contemplated how to use her treasures.

She'd booked an Airbnb with a second-floor terrace, and the color of the sky at sunset enthralled me. During the day, we checked out the vendors, sorting smoky-quartz cabochons, finding great sterling chains and small raw blue diamonds. By night, we laughed, drank lots of wine, ate good food, and cried together over the ways that our marriages had been painful. She was recently separated, and her divorce was still in the raw, blistered stage. Our time together was a glorious salve for our wounded hearts.

My thoughts silently mirrored hers as she marveled at and was fearful of what might be next in her new single life. Mostly, she was hopeful, even looking at cute bungalows wondering if it would be prudent to invest in a rental property. I simply basked in the wonder of the mountains and the glow of friendship.

COVID had come into the world's awareness by then but was not yet raging in the United States, and we naively assumed the outbreak would be contained. Assumed, with the arrogance of Americans, that it would not affect us.

We returned to our homes happy and fortified by the friendship, but it wasn't long after that trip that COVID began its insidious, terrifying creep into our lives, and no one could assume they would be spared.

The Naples condo that had once held such promise had become a bitter tomb reeking of an ugly past, so we moved north to St. Petersburg, Florida, purchasing a downtown condo on the water and infusing our new marriage with a new home.

We were settled then. Enjoying the energy of walking out the door of our building to restaurants, the movie theater, or the marina. But the norm of life began to wither as COVID put the world on pause. Confusion and fear preoccupied me, along with the hunt for disinfectant, toilet paper, and the sewing of masks. The wonderful high that sustained me after my trip was shoved to the back of my memory bank, hopefully to be revisited when normalcy returned in a matter of a few weeks or months.

Survival kit secured, I needed to find a way to exist, to return to the work of daily life despite the crisis. Gluing myself to the television or social media for the latest infection numbers or death counts, while seemingly necessary, would not calm my anxiety or frustrations. Instead, I haltingly turned back to writing and art. I had three novels out in the world by then, and the fourth was due in just a few months. Revisions inched painfully along as the harsh reality of body bag shortages, temporary morgues, and daily devastation with no end in sight crowded out my desire to explore death on the pages of fiction.

Painting became my lifeline. Since I was no longer able to have coffee with friends or go out to lunch at one of the local restaurants, my beautiful apartment was becoming a cave I was afraid to leave. Not long before I'd traveled to Tucson, I'd rented a painting studio in an old school being repurposed as a workspace for creatives. As the first and only tenant, the risk to my health while in the building was minimal and the decision quickly seemed prescient. There, I could lose myself in color and marks, letting my creative instincts and the physicality of my brushstrokes take away any lingering worry. I felt normal and free, putting the uncertainty of the future on a shelf for two days a week. There, I had a place to breathe.

Like many, I found the raging pandemic all-consuming, and plans of any kind were increasingly hard to make. Commitments long on the calendar were broken as the reality of timing and infection rates growing at an alarming rate dictated. Writing conferences and painting retreats that had been on my schedule were pushed back to the fall. Certainly, all would be back to normal by then.

As snowbirds, my husband and I cloistered ourselves in our Florida condo, fearing travel, until the governor abandoned mask policies in bars and restaurants. One trip to a local restaurant to pick up takeout, where no one, including waitstaff, wore masks, became our breaking point. Chicago seemed a safer bet given the city's politics, so we braved the airport and moved back north.

In Chicago, there were few mask-less people even on the streets. Indoor dining was shut down. Our condo building had appropriate restrictions. COVID protocols were simply taken with appropriate seriousness, and we forged a new routine. We took walks, used our balcony, had groceries delivered, and attempted to live life while staying safe.

But I'd lost my private painting space, and the walls began to close in on me.

PART II

CHAPTER ELEVEN
INFECTIOUS SADNESS

Dead woman walking.

I don't know what this void is that I feel. I can't name it or describe it or categorize it, other than to call it an infectious sadness replicating in my cells. Pieces of empty longing have converged and become more than the sum of my parts, robbing me of my core like a leech, feeding off my blood, growing bigger and stronger, threatening to take control.

Why is it there? What does it want of me?

We're months into COVID isolation now. The days are full of worry and caution; optimism, a distant memory; plans for the future, futile. We watch the infection rate and body count rise unrestrained. The easy explanation would be to attribute my fragile emotional state to the uncertainty and endlessness of the ravages of the virus. Some call it COVID depression. Sometimes I do too. I even hope that's what it is, because then there will be an end to it. Masking, distancing, and an eventual vaccine will return life to what it had been, we're told.

But for now, infectious-disease experts speculate about time frames months out. Terms such as *herd immunity* and *R-naught* and *PPE* pepper the nightly news. Images of refrigerated semitrailers parked outside of New York City hospitals acting as overflow morgues are burned into our memories. Politicians grandstand, agencies fail us, basic medical supplies, such as masks, are rare and precious, and individuals place selfishness above all, leaving little to comfort me.

Although not prone to depression, I intellectually recognize this anguish as such, having been shredded once before. But it's been several years, and there has been no new devastation. So why now? The fragile threads of my marriage seem to be holding. We've rebuilt, I think.

No, that isn't accurate. We've forged something different from the ashes after my husband burned it to the ground.

I'm restricted, yes, but my health and the health of my family have been untouched by the pandemic thus far. Our financial resources are secure, my loved ones are safe and equally cautious. To be depressed over being locked in my beautiful apartment feels shallow and entitled when so many have real suffering.

So, what is the source of my anguish?

Perhaps the awareness of my approaching birthday, a big one, has been creeping in, affecting my sense of self? But I hadn't panicked in the past when an age ending in a zero hit. There has been no lamenting, no regret, no coddling of my mind or my body or my attitude. Is this birthday hitting me the way I'm told big birthdays are supposed to hit women? With fear and surrender, and assumptions that relevance and beauty and sexuality no longer apply?

That, too, feels false; I feel none of that. I'm healthy and vibrant—youthful in all the ways society judges women. I do not long to be thirty again. But I can no longer contain or deny the discomfort within me, regardless of its source. It needs a place to go, a place outside my heart and my head. I need to release it into the world, because the pain of holding it in has become too great. But so is the fear.

Fear of what? Knowing the answer?

Underneath, where I'm afraid to dwell, I sense the magnitude of this destructive force I can't name. Like a dolphin sensing an impending hurricane, I seek a safe place in deeper waters. But will there be a price to pay?

In rational moments, I remind myself that I'm a grown-ass woman who should be able to sort through the emotions wreaking havoc on her life. But I am blindsided and without answers.

Whatever it is, instead of celebrating, today I'm driven to find a release, to find a place where my thoughts and my frustrations and my fears and my pain can run free from this confinement. I haven't said any of this out loud, haven't confided in a friend, or poured my heart out to my husband. I'm not ready to expose my vulnerability. Instead, I feel the need to sit with my own thoughts, to sort through my feelings privately because I can't yet articulate the source of the pain.

Nor can I put its urgency into perspective

This birthday should be a day of warmth, love, and pleasant thoughts for the future. Confinement has robbed me of a planned celebratory trip to Spain, leaving in its place a day where the emptiness of my current life is simply magnified.

But my husband has given me a lovely, thoughtful gift. A ring. I'd chosen the stone on my trip to Tucson with my friend Ann during the Gem Show, just before COVID changed our world. I'd asked her to design something for me with the lovely yellow sapphire. She did but then conspired with my husband to present it as a gift from him, rather than the gift I had intended to give to myself. It was kind and thoughtful and beautiful of both of them.

Although I love the ring, it's also a reminder that the trip was one of the last days where I've felt free and happy and uncaged. That trip and Tucson, with the fascinating way the light played on the mountains, loom large in my mind, and I vow to return. But it isn't clear if my longing is for the place or for the experience of unfettered time with a friend whom I sorely miss.

Tears have been just below the surface for hours now. My heart is heavy when it shouldn't be. I feel guilty and helpless and selfish and, at moments, hopeless. I can't sort through the symptoms, the feelings of emptiness and longing, to understand their source. Without that, how do I proceed?

The world is burning, literally and figuratively, and I have no right to be selfish and petty when so many are truly in despair, but my need is there, nonetheless.

And I'm brought back to the question I cannot answer: What is cause and what is effect?

The warping of time is an odd side effect of COVID isolation. Without the calendar markers of appointments or meetings, days of the week blur. Past and present converge.

Bits of our history—the ugly stage of my marriage—again pop into my thoughts unbidden. They'd been there, partially buried, surfacing every so often—though less frequently as time went on—like shards of glass just beneath the sand. The sudden sting is strong; the hurt dished out, so crushing. I wondered if I'd feel it always.

Without the distraction of the outside world, desolation has torn open a new void, one that seems harder to define. A general malaise.

An emptiness that leaves me flat. *Am I going back to that place where the wound is raw and oozing?* The thought sits rancid in my gut, knotting my chest, pulsing blood loudly in my veins.

The broken sleep that had been a hallmark of that time of pain has come back. I spend hours staring at the ceiling in the early hours of the morning, listening to the creaks and moans of a high-rise condo building, and my husband breathing loudly beside me. I toss and turn, unable to get comfortable. I punch my pillows, throw my bedding on and off, seeking a place or position more conducive to sleep. My mind runs wild with questions, amorphous in their lack of specificity.

I run through the list of obvious sleep aides: I swap out my pillow for something that is supposed to cradle my head more effectively. I increase my melatonin. I add CBD to my nighttime routine. Nothing changes the outcome. Yet, I'm loath to leave our bed, knowing that if my husband wakes and finds me gone, he, too, will recognize symptoms of our ugly past and assume that I've sunk back into that pit where my mind will not release me.

It is hard to define the cause of my sleeplessness. And I certainly can't in the dark at three a.m. Thoughts of our history float through my mind, but it is an emptiness that I'm feeling more than hurt and anger. I can't put words to the undefinable emotions or explain what I feel beyond concluding it must be related to the COVID pandemic. My self-diagnosis is a logical conclusion under the circumstances—the entire world is at collective risk for mental health crises. Eventually, after weeks of crushing deprivation, I heed my body and get out of bed, moving into the living room.

Isn't that what sleep experts recommend for "good sleep hygiene?" Get up if you're not sleeping. Go to bed at a routine time. Use your bed for sleep and sex, nothing more. Blah, blah, blah.

Okay. I'll try.

Silently, I turn back the covers and slip out, tiptoeing out of the room. I find my robe and park my sleepless self in another darkened room where I simply stare at new things, night after night.

Again, I pour over the rawness of the old hurts in the middle of the night as I gaze at the moon over Lake Michigan, alone and out of sorts but now with a more analytic lens. I sort the pieces into buckets for consideration, hoping to understand where the emptiness comes from. COVID's control and our fears of it are layered into the mix, where I dissect and rearrange all the information. Hoping, I suppose, that one day my naturally analytic mind will be able to fully separate his illness and his emptiness from the consequences inflicted on me, and then I can banish them from my mind.

I want it gone. I want to exist in a place where these wrenching memories hold no sway, want to exorcise the pain seemingly fused to my cells. He is sober now. He is honoring his promises.

But now, an emptiness resides in me.

As the sleepless nights drone on and months stretch beyond comprehension with no clear end in sight, one thing repeatedly creeps in from the shadows: an awareness of the extent to which I'm living numb. It is as if my heart and the deepest sense of myself and my own desires have been frozen in a block of ice so solid I can't feel much of anything anymore. My emotions seem largely encased where they can't be touched. Any feelings that make their way through the mantel are fleeting, surface-level affairs, and I navigate the world like a new-found version of a Stepford wife. Not with pumped-up boobs and a prissy wardrobe, but by doing and saying what is expected of me.

I'm on autopilot. "Everything is fine. Don't I look fine? Don't I sound fine?"

I know how to wear the mask of normalcy. I've learned it like all good little girls do, step by cautious step over a lifetime. My smile isn't as bright anymore; my laugh, not as easy. The warmth that would normally radiate from me during my interactions with the world is dialed down, but the world hasn't noticed.

Hell, I hadn't noticed until recently.

Occasionally my husband asks if I'm okay, but it is always some momentary low mood he is asking about, some mood that dips below my recent numb baseline. I brush it off, saying I'm just tired or tired of the isolation, knowing there is some other unidentifiable ache. In other moments, when I'm feeling more forlorn, I admit a general, undefined sadness has hit me—the COVID blues showing their hand. Inevitably, the response sparks the briefest of conversations. A word or two, nothing more. But a deeper conversation never comes. There are no probing questions about why it's happening or what it means, but to be fair, I don't think I've been able or willing to answer truthfully. I don't yet know that either.

But does he want to know the truth?

I suppose it should have occurred to me to question whether I wanted to be asked, to be truly heard and understood, but it hasn't before now. I guess the answer is both. Yes, because I would have viewed the questions as a demonstration of love and concern for my mental health. No, because I simply don't have answers to my own truth. My heart and my deepest emotions are still buried deep down in that solid, frozen cube.

Like a beetle flash-frozen in a lake, I can see my outline if I look closely—the rough edges and ridges of my former self. But my heart has worked long and hard to protect itself from further damage, and the accumulated scar tissue feels impenetrable.

Objectivity requires distance, and there is no distance when you're mired in the thick of an all-consuming survival event. I hadn't thought of the last few years of my life that way until COVID forced it to the surface. A survival event. Three simple words that describe what I've been through as succinctly as possible. I've been fighting for survival, for emotional survival—his first and then my own.

"Is numbness the price I have to pay? Is a half-existence my lot in life?" I ask myself for the first time.

I've been so focused on the tasks of saving a life, then saving myself from collapse, then saving a marriage, that the future of me has been absent.

CHAPTER TWELVE
NUMBNESS

Sitting at breakfast in the morning with my husband, in awe over our Lake Michigan views, I look across the table with love. Aware of his hard work, aware of the effort he's made every day to show me he is a better man now and his demons have been chased away, I'm grateful for everything we have.

I look at him, remembering how this simple act of seeing his face and hearing his voice would fill me, make me go soft with love more than two decades into our marriage. Love is still present, but its light burns dimmer and a simple glance no longer fills me. Emotions are blunted. The intensity of my love has faded; my adoration, wiped away by his lies, but the memory of our old love now haunts me, and I wish for the ghost that roams in my heart.

As my nightly emotional postmortem drags on without end, I exist in a shatterproof terrarium, watching the world outside as if I am simply part of a science experiment. My body is confused about night and day. My mind is confused about emotions I cannot tap. Sleeplessness dulls me, swallowing me into nothingness, leaving me teetering again on the edge of an abyss.

And then, there's a new light. A beam. A quickening of my breath. A distraction. An infatuation. Another man.

I didn't recognize it at the moment it started. I simply noticed his voice, his kind eyes, his steady strength. Something about this man hit me, striking me hard.

As time drifts forward, elusive and fragmented, and I'm alone with my barren emptiness, this man sparks something deep, something I'd forgotten myself capable of: desire.

This blinding preoccupation is for a stranger, a man I've never met. A public figure I've been aware of for quite some time. I had certainly found him smart and attractive, but how has he come to consume my thoughts? Why? Why now?

Infatuation had moved into obsession.

First, he began to enter my dreams. Casually and infrequently, but consistently. They were dreams of tenderness, then urgency, then passion.

The dreams were a comfort when I woke at three a.m. restless and sleepless. He became my companion as I stared at the ceiling longing for something vague but urgent, eventually lulling me back to sleep with his whispered promises.

Then, he became a need.

Now, he has inserted himself into my waking reality where fantasies fill my day when other interests can't.

Is it emptiness that allows this obsession to flourish, or has the emptiness always been present and is now revealed because it no longer has cover?

I escape to my office for most of the day, purportedly to write, but words won't come. My manuscript holds no interest. I dawdle and find

134

distractions and fritter away hours that disappear into the ether, time I can't account for because my mind won't stay grounded. It's as if I've lost the skill of complex thought or focus. I try, day after day, to get words on the page, to complete the outline of my next novel, but my head won't stay in the work, the effort is simply beyond my ability to focus.

Fueled by sleep deprivation, it is the emptiness, the why of it, the why of the obsession, the need for answers that instead consume me.

Why plot a novel when I can escape with a nap, slipping into the lusciousness that has become my imaginary life? How can I find words when the temptation of this man's eyes haunts me? Why feel the emptiness when I can feel longing?

But the disrupted sleep wears on my body. The hours in the middle of the night remain a desolate void. Some nights, I'm so exhausted, so wired but tired, I can't even quiet my mind enough to slip into the dreams. Instead, I crash back into my favorite spot on the couch in midafternoon, creating a cycle doomed to repeat itself.

But why is he here?

I've been in this place before, not this place of blind desire, but where sleeplessness destroys health, where skin is sallow, hair begins to fall, and brain fog sets in. And I know the consequences awaiting me. But the cycle will not break. Is my sleeplessness mental or physical? Or all things wrapped into one?

But I didn't retreat into fantasies of another man then. Why have I done so now?

Yet I need the obsession. I need those magnetic eyes. I need to vanish into a different place, a different time. I crave it. Over and over I create images of how we'd meet. Feeling that first touch. That first kiss. The lusciousness of bare flesh, and I'm lost in it.

I've never lived in my imagination like this. I've never been consumed by a fabricated life, a fabricated person. I am not impulsive or reckless or careless. This is not me. But yet, suddenly, it is.

I have no illusions that these fantasies have one iota of possibility behind them, nor am I certain that I'd even want it to be real. The fantasies confuse me and comfort me, adding to the battered stew that is my heart and my head.

Again, why he is here? The question haunts me as much as the imagined trail of heat his fingers leave on my skin. Is he a consequence of the relentless isolation or the loss of the alone time I seem to need? Maybe it's loss of my other creative outlet, the physical one: painting. Where I can be bold and intuitive and rarely prone to distraction. Perhaps too much togetherness with my husband after so much time apart is the cause. It could be the need to have something to look forward to after having been deprived of ordinary dreams. Or is it simply a crutch to get me through the unprecedented hell of COVID? Perhaps there is something else I haven't yet considered that's turned what would've been a lovely, sweet infatuation that would have faded into a raging compulsion.

The obsession weighs on me. Futile questions of why flash through my mind in the early morning hours between dreams until I brush them away, too, and retreat back to the lusciousness. This fantasy feels both unhealthy and as necessary as breathing.

One afternoon, as I let my body surrender to a nap while my mind imagines eyes lush with desire locked on mine and a mouth gliding across silky skin, my eyes jolt open with another thought. *Does my obsession serve a purpose beyond distraction?* I've assumed a cause-and-effect relationship, but should I be considering its purpose? Does it serve me?

Is it revenge?

A fantasy affair because I won't have a real one—don't have the courage to have one. And my husband has made me hate that about myself. He didn't deserve my loyalty and should not expect it now.

But I am not him.

I miss painting. The feel of a lush, sloppy brush as it glides across the canvas. The way a surprise drip or an errant mark can shift perspective. The way layers and history transform and inform, reveal and shape. I miss the unbridled physicality of it. For me, painting is all instinct and response to things I can't always describe. It's free and loose and takes me away from any thoughts outside of the piece I'm working on.

Standing in front of a blank canvas, I load a brush and am excited about that first mark. Nothing is a mistake. There are no wrong colors or poor choices of line. Each mark is simply the foundation for the layers that come after and the layers after that, building, refining, allowing one turn of the brush to inform a decision about the next. Painting is instinct now; the foundation elements of color and form and proportion are deeply embedded in who I am through my training and history in the apparel industry. Writing, a more recent skill, does not always flow unconsciously. Words must be dragged into existence and only provide a place to lose myself when the work is close to its final form and I can see the story as it has unfolded.

Painting can remove me from the emptiness if I let it.

Here, in my Chicago apartment, I don't have the space to get messy. I've stolen a corner of a spare bedroom as a dedicated painting space, but even with plastic tacked up covering the drywall, I'm constrained by pretty walls and pretty floors and things I don't want mussed up.

Here my work is small and tight, lacking boldness. Another metaphor perhaps?

An in-person drawing workshop I was scheduled to attend has been reconfigured because of COVID. Art via Zoom.

Rectangles of heavy paper have been trimmed to size with their edges taped. Thirty sit stacked awaiting the first streak of color. Charcoal and pencils and blenders and all manner of mark-making tools are organized on my stainless-steel table, and my computer is propped nearby so I can both watch and draw.

Excitement and disappointment compete for attention. Disappointment is simply a result of losing the immersion that comes from working in a magical creative space. I start with a piece of pressed charcoal as fat as a carrot and push it across the paper, watching the dust trail add its own pattern. I grab the blender, then an eraser, then tackle the paper with my bare fingers, moving the graphite from one sheet to another. Finding my rhythm. Finding composition. Losing myself again.

Hour after hour, I hide in this spare room, moving pigments around. Working small but pushing myself to be bold with my marks, trying to use the constraints of size and time. Again, joy shuts out the emptiness and my obsession goes back on the shelf, tucked away for a time later when the void will reappear.

Three days in, one of the instructors, aware that I'm an author, challenges me to include words in my pieces. I sit with the idea, not immediately drawn to it. Then I pick up a pencil and write the word *obsession*. Then a swath of paint, oil pastels, more pencil, and the word is obscured.

I've embedded a secret.

A flood of words and phrases pop into my head. Emotions, fears, and desires become lodged in the work, hidden or hinted at. Titles, never easy for me, roll into my mind even before a piece has been conceived of. Instead of painful afterthoughts, two dozen titles are waiting for paintings.

Titles that can hold my secrets and inspire the painting to do the same.

Tentatively, I mark new paper, each word an expression of pain or wants or fears, but I bury the message, hiding it under washes of paint and smears of charcoal. The vulnerability of my words is too obvious for me to release. Each small piece becomes a visual journal holding testament to my emotional state, containing the code, I hope, that might release my emptiness.

Or is it simply another way to hide my true self in the shadows? Another silent scream?

————————

There are days I feel like a fraud.

And days I feel like a stalker.

It's hard to remember how long it's been since I've had a night without waking when the room is dark, when time is ambiguous. I alternate in those early morning hours between my deepest loneliness and the joy of the reprieve from emptiness as I replant myself unfettered into the obsession that has taken control of my mind.

Or is it in my heart?

What's real, what's fantasy, and what's memory all converge as I place myself desperately into a setting where I can feel something again. Day after day, it becomes harder, the numbness screaming, "Look at me!" My confidence that this is simply some stage of COVID depression that will pass and life will return to normal is waning. It seems deeper, as if it's trying to shake me awake or, if I'm not careful, slap me until I'm again bruised and battered.

How do I separate circumstances from desires? Is this loneliness, this craving a result of constriction? Of the seemingly endless confinement? Or is it, perhaps, a fear that I'll never again feel the passion betrayal has robbed me of? Has confinement created the emptiness or simply held a mirror up to it?

During wakeful moments, I remain confused, reading into things when I can't be sure what they mean, assigning importance to small actions and nonevents because my own thoughts are unreliable narrators. But what conclusion should I draw from my husband's lack of interest in my recent trouble with sleep, his lack of curiosity about my repeatedly stated sadness, or from his tentative inquiries into my emotional state or my commitment to our relationship that are only done at night as my body is crashing and serious discussion is impossible?

There is one and only one conclusion I can draw: he's afraid to hear my answers.

And I need this obsession the way I need air. I need him during the hours in the dark when I'm lost in the fantasy. Although they are torturous at moments, I relish the way I feel when those desires consume me. I relish feeling something again, anything that isn't pain. But what does that mean? What do I do about it? Do I *need* to do something about it?

What questions would a therapist ask? She'd ask what I would do if, by some miracle, there were a real choice to be made about this fabricated man and the fabricated relationship I'm having with him. The ludicrousness of the scenario stops me with its absurdity, forcing my brain to seize up.

Then I have another thought. Perhaps, once again, I'm waiting for someone else to force my hand. Do I want my husband to tire of my numbness and indecision? Do I want him to be the one to leave?

Should I have left long ago? The question has periodically rumbled under the surface since we reconciled. In my dark moments, I replay our past with new words and outcomes. I mime "if only I had" or "I wish I had." I wonder what swallowing that bitter pill feels like. The thing unsaid. The thing not done. I know people who live their lives consumed by blame and regret in connection to some old hurt until it rots them from the inside and they are bloated and toxic with their pain. We all do.

Is that what's happening to me? I tell myself I'm waiting for clarity. But what if clarity never comes? Isn't that my real fear? Is that why the obsession is here? Is that the purpose of my fascination with this man, and the reason I'm living in this made up place?

Has he dropped into my life to hold my hand while I finally set aside the indecision that tears at my heart for once and for all?

But how can any emotion in a place of obsession be anything other than false? The visceral reaction I'm having—projecting character and behaviors onto a man who is little more than an avatar—disturbs and confuses me, which in itself shows me the fragility of my mind even if I'm not so sick I can't recognize the irrationality.

Instinct has rarely failed me. But when it has, the fail has been epic. The one huge failure of trust I had placed in my husband is something I may never recover from, but was that my failure or the mastery of the liar?

Again, I am that mess grasping at breath—a lighter version, a functional version, but a mess nonetheless. But outward appearances don't give me away. I'm not curled up on the floor or passing out from stress;

instead, I'm floating through life as if watching it from someplace else, not letting it touch me.

I pick up the phone to call the therapist. I need help. I can't see through the numbness or around it or past it.

I hang up on the first ring, my heart racing with dread.

A call to a therapist will mean an end to my obsession. And the thought of losing it, even when I know it's intruding on reality, is more than I can endure.

The fantasies are a comfort—the one comfort I can count on and can control. In them, I can feel again, can lose myself in something that makes my heart race and unleashes the torrent of emotions I have trapped under the surface with no outlet. Inevitably, they remind me that I cannot act. There is nothing here but an imaginary world created out of desire. So the emptiness craters me again. And the cycle repeats.

The obsession is just a symptom. A symptom of what, I don't know.

But for now, I need it. I need him.

At first pass, it would be simple to say this obsession is about sex, but I don't think so. Sex is the byproduct, although that isn't a full answer either.

This is about desire, I realize. The need to feel desired, the need to feel desire myself, because that too has gone numb. This isn't about sex.

It's about want and tenderness and heat.

It's about wanting to live without the baggage and hurt from the past.

It's about the fear that my current state of numbness is all I have left.

Wrapped in confusion and feeling a therapist is unsafe, I decide on another course: a journal. I'll write. I'll sort through the insanity of my emotions on paper. These feelings rage within me, bouncing from longing to despair with no place to land, wringing my insides like a swath of *shibori* silk twisted and wrapped around a pole.

Aside from junior high and the brief "this is what the jackass did" stint during our attempt at divorce, I have not been a journaler. The risk of committing my most private, painful thoughts to paper was unthinkable. After all, journals are real things that can be found in a drawer. They can be read by people you don't want to read them, or read at a time you're too vulnerable to address their contents. And ironically, a history of snooping is there in my marriage. Texts have been read. Emails have been read. Jealousy has been an undercurrent through much of our relationship. Unleashing the rawest of emotions in a tangible form had been inconceivable until it became the only option I saw.

A journal feels passive-aggressive now, I think. Perhaps I want my thoughts exposed. Perhaps I want my husband to know my longing and for the thorn of pain to sink in and fester inside him the way it has for me. I tell myself that I'm simply adopting a practical option. In the middle of COVID, a visit with a therapist means Zoom. Another cold, unemotional exchange with a stranger who would prod me with questions I know I can't answer yet.

I've been down that road before; I know the drill. "How does that make you feel? What do you think it means? What would you do if . . . ?" I don't feel ready to answer the real questions or deal with the "why" underneath it all that therapy is ultimately trying to unearth. Or maybe my apprehension is another avoidance.

Instead of talking to a shrink, I approach the task of exploring my malaise and the accompanying obsession the way I would one of my novels. I'll open a journal—an old-fashioned paper version—to use as my dirty first draft. The one no one will ever see. First drafts are full of flat rhetoric that allows you to explore the story you want to tell or random words that are trashed once released. If you're lucky, there will be nuggets of insight that need to be turned inside out like a puzzle. Perhaps the act of release, of committing words to a page, will be all I will need to let myself loose of the anguish and uncertainty binding me.

I walk down to Paper Source. No drugstore volume will do. There, I choose a black Moleskine. It's writerly and fits well in my hand. The hardcover is appropriately serious for the importance of the task. The smooth paper is luxurious as it holds the lead of the Paper Mate pencils I prefer. And its size is suitable for being tucked into or behind things should I need to conceal it.

The first entry tumbles out of me, three pages of rambling emotional confusion. It's awkward at first, then the spigot opens and words flow in a torrent without judgment. Some days, only a sentence graces the page, others hold swaths of blistering, disjointed text.

Pages and pages bounce through the tumult of free-form questions that consume me. I let the words spill out, not taking time to process or judge their meaning, but it's in here somewhere. I feel it. If I ask enough, if I turn these emotions over, add heat and light, they will compost into something rich and life-sustaining.

Memories of the therapist who had suggested journaling as I struggled to comprehend my husband's infidelity come rushing back. She hadn't pushed to understand my fears of documenting my grief. And I hadn't given consideration to the elements of that conversation that had been missing. Why had she not explored my fear of discovery and what it could have meant to me and my healing?

Time has given me a new lens. My terror was rooted in my fear of dealing with the full extent of the problem. My refusal to write these things down, to document my truths, was about exposure. I was afraid of facing the full, ugly reality and the consequences of my own devastation. I can see that now, in ways so incredibly obvious for the first time. I was doing my own compartmentalization, protecting my own fragile psyche.

Perhaps because I'm an author now, the idea of exposing myself on the page is less terrifying. Perhaps the distance from the event has helped. I'm not sure, nor does it really matter. But for whatever reason, I am now compelled to document every ugly, needy, vulnerable, and delicious emotion. I need some method to get these feelings out of my head and to explore the obsessive thoughts that have taken over my mind, my body, and my heart.

It's a new way to be heard. This time by the most important person: me. There is no longer value in burying the whole in the small parts.

———————————

"Are you living with your trauma, or have you become your trauma?" The question popped into my Twitter feed today as a random meme intended to provoke conversation, I suppose.

I've always thought of trauma as something sharp and obvious. Whether a single unmistakable incident or a series of events; it left you decimated and, therefore, was impossible to ignore. Now, processing the emptiness inside me and searching for answers to its source, I'm beginning to consider another paradigm—the subtle impact of chronic trauma.

The trauma of my husband's secret life was undeniable. It laid me flat, shattering the core of my existence. But were his years of boozing a trauma as well?

Consumed with thoughts of what he was doing to himself, searching for ways to hold a mirror up to his self-destruction, fearing for the damage he was causing my family, the person largely left out of the equation was me. I was at the center of it all, moment by moment switching roles—coach, referee, or cheerleader—but my focus was on everyone else. I existed on the fringes.

The messages of Al-Anon and the messages from Family Week at the rehab center play back in my mind. Our healing was relegated to attitude adjustment. "Stop blaming yourself. You did not cause his drinking. You cannot cure him. Let's talk about the twenty-five ways you are enabling him." While attitude may be the starting point, it alone will not restore emotional stability lost in the battle for sobriety.

What if all that is left now is a memory of the me that once existed?

CHAPTER THIRTEEN
RING IS OFF

The claustrophobia of COVID, even while locked in a beautiful Chicago condo, has left us both snippy and irritated. I haven't seen my kids or my sister or my elderly father for over ten months. So we take the risk, pack up the car and the cat, and drive up to the family lake house six hours north. Northern Wisconsin is brazenly oblivious to the ravages of the pandemic, but we can stock the fridge with food, and isolate ourselves from humanity while listening to the loons and hoping for a glimpse of a bald eagle or a family of otters. My husband can fish from the kayak. I can read from the deck. And Isabel can dream of the chipmunks that taunt her from the opposite side of a porch screen.

Despite his age and rocky health, my father has joined his neighbors in believing COVID "won't happen here." We're wearing masks when he arrives at the house to join us for dinner.

"Oh, do I need a mask?" he asks.

I usher him out to the deck, make him an old-fashioned, and we all sit outside eating pan-fried fresh-caught bass and corn on the cob as if nothing in our world has changed. The virus hasn't impacted him or anyone he knows here in this small town, and they remain locked in belief that it never will.

We spend two weeks living as if COVID is somewhere else, a distant threat, isolated as we are from other people and scary news. Nothing can go wrong when waves lap gently on the shore, sunsets blaze red, and loons send their sweet calls through the pines.

My husband is scheduled to give a Zoom lecture to a graduate class two days before we return to Chicago. He's determined the internet here is unreliable, so he rents a car and drives back to Chicago while I stay to have a little more time with my dad.

Not long after he leaves, I impulsively slip off my wedding ring. I stare at the spot on my finger, seeing the shift in the color of my skin, the slight indentation in my flesh that brands me. I live without it, testing the feel of it. This is my time to ponder my place in the world and what I desire.

I suppose I'm just testing whether it feels as foreign to be without it now as it had in the past. Normally, the missing metal, even for an hour of cleaning, would have been a beacon screaming at me with its absence. Now I gaze at the bare flesh and feel nothing.

Here alone, thoughts of Tucson pop back into my mind. I ache for the comfort I felt on that trip at the beginning of the year. Was it the serenity of the place or the time spent with a friend? Can I tell the difference now when I'm distanced from both?

Would the serenity return if I lived there? If I lived there alone?

I stare at the strange, naked spot on my finger without answers. I'm confused, empty, and in need of something to remind me I'm alive. That trip, many months in the past now, was the last time I felt my heart sing.

Normally, the Northwoods is a place of calm, quiet recharging for me. Hours are spent staring at the lake and the ducks, tossing apples to the deer, inhaling the heady scent of pine, listening to the sounds of the night. It brings back fond childhood memories of climbing trees and catching frogs, swimming in ice-cold water, biking for miles. But this time, my emptiness and longing are magnified. Despite the beauty and solitude, I can't find contentment.

Thinking a diversion would help, I sit on the deck, my feet planted on an ottoman, and open a new novel. My choice quickly appears ill-advised. In it, the protagonist describes his obsession with a woman other than his wife in words so familiar my heart aches. Then, pages later, the lover taunts him, asking if his wife holds the same power over him. I toss the book aside, abruptly shoved into the past, into a different reality, into hurt, then walk the narrow side roads near the house until my feet rebel.

My obsessive dreams have been difficult to process here even while alone. I want them, want their comfort, but my mind stays stuck in a scene, replaying it on a loop. I still can't grapple with what I'm supposed to do with these feelings. How am I supposed to move forward? How am I supposed to set this aside and find a way through this to something healthy?

The intention and reality of my obsession confuse me. Every detail is so real. I can conjure up a look, a touch, a conversation, and most importantly, the way it makes me feel. The warmth washes over me in ways nothing else does now. The way nothing has for a very long time. I want it so badly—need it so badly. Need it to feel alive. Need it to breathe. Need it to keep from collapsing in despair.

I can live in this obsession, or I can wither and die of loneliness and emptiness. It's the numbness that is hardest to stomach. Maybe because I've been numb for so long. Numb, I now realize, since I learned my marriage had been a lie.

Is that what's going on? The numbness, the shock that nothing in my life was what it seemed, is it finally abating? Is this hitting me so hard because I can finally feel something? Because I finally want something?

Now I'm forced to face myself. Forced to deal with the reality of my damaged heart. There are no distractions here. I can't bury my truth under busyness or activities or friends. I can only hold the mirror up to myself and question my heart. Or I could try to pull the heavy cloak of denial back over my head.

Back at the house that evening, I return to the chair on the deck and pop in headphones. On the recommendation of a friend, I've downloaded Glennon Doyle's *Untamed*. The irony of being pushed to read Doyle, whose own marriage included serial infidelity, is not lost on me. I never told my friend, the one who presented me with the suggestion, what I'd been through—at least not the unvarnished version. I've still told no one the full story. Bits and pieces, yes, but I've kept the full, ugly truth hidden. I'm ashamed of it.

I'm ashamed of myself.

It's not my husband's failings but my own that shame me.

I've never thought of myself as a woman who puts up with disrespect. It's not how the world views me, but despite my on-again, off-again, file for divorce, I've stayed. Stayed because I believed the love was deep enough to overcome the hurt—the after.

I stayed because I knew the work my husband had done to understand and fix himself and to repair the damage was worthy of love. Worthy of respect. After all, he'd done it for me. He'd done it to earn back a place in my life, and I believed that alone would eventually bring me back to a place of love, trust, and respect if we gave it the time and care it required.

But my husband's hypocrisy has been as deep and as painful and as hard to live with as his betrayal.

Perhaps it's the hypocrisy now in me as I lust for another man, even one I've fabricated, that leaves me unsettled.

My obsession is the first time I've wanted another man, *really* wanted another man since I married. I've certainly thought about sex, including revenge sex, but this is the first time a man has lit me up, pushing my buttons.

I have to remind myself constantly that the obsession is a fantasy, that the aspects I've attributed to this man are things I've projected onto him, taking cues from his public persona. I've fabricated the man I want to exist, the man I want to distract me with his attention. Yet the insanity of those thoughts is also never far from the surface. It feels right to me in one moment; the next, I'm looking for a padded room. Other moments, I feel I'm in waiting. That something is going to happen, something unknown, something I can't define or describe because to do so would expose the absurdity. Is this obsession something intended to spur me forward while I wait for some unknown prize the universe will drop in my lap if I'm patient? Or has it presented itself as a technique to help me release the glue holding me hostage?

Right now, my obsession is the object I desire. Crazy or not, it's the only object I can see.

And. I. Want. It.

Little by little, I see a glimmer of truth in the words I've written furtively on blank journal pages. Words that gel, revealing a pattern. Words that feel true deep in my gut. The haze over the purpose of my obsession is lifting, showing its form.

I see it now. I see why he's here. He's a mirror here to show me I'm not done healing. To show me the depth of the damage that still exists. To show me the parts of me that have been in hibernation: numb, sheltered, drained. He's showing me where I've been self-protective, holding back parts of my heart because I've been afraid of being hurt again.

Through these long, lonely months of fantasy, he has cast focus on parts of my very identity that have been missing, reigniting desire and longing. He is allowing me to consider the possibility that someone else could, perhaps, show me love without the hurt.

He's showing me myself as I might exist without the weight of betrayal.

I don't consider myself unlovable or undesirable or unworthy. But I've changed. I'm a shell of what I had been, simply too drained to feel. My husband didn't cheat because our passion had waned or he no longer found me beautiful or I had "let myself go" or any of the other ridiculous excuses adulterers concoct to justify their bad behavior. But the hole in him has become a hole in me, no longer able to hold the essence of the woman who once held joy.

I am still collateral damage. His pain has left me discarded in a heap on the floor, emotionally empty and questioning everything I ever believed to be true about myself and my world. His betrayal, after nearly two decades of me fighting for his sobriety and putting his needs over mine, was the ultimate destruction.

Love is the greatest gift one human being gives to another, and my gift was discarded.

152

I no longer know who I am as numbness confines me to the shadows, burying me in the fog of pain.

Men over fifty in the available dating pool fall into three camps:

Divorced, which means they're angry at a wife who left them or they're cheaters. Cheaters now angry because they have to live with the consequences enacted by a skilled attorney who ripped them apart and left them soothing their bruised egos with a string of way-too-young women barely older than their daughters.

Widowed, which means they're sad and pining for lost love or looking for a housekeeper/companion that they can call wife number two. Or they're trying to make lemonade out of the situation by being a player, because that's what they think men of a certain age are supposed to do while the equipment still works.

Last, we have the never married. This, frankly, seems like the worst group. A grown-ass man who's spent his entire life avoiding commitment, compromise, negotiation, and true emotional attachment. No way in hell do I need another relationship where I become the emotional-intelligence coach. I already have that T-shirt.

But it's not like I'm jaded or anything. Nor do I know what the hell I'm talking about since I haven't been "out there," to borrow a phrase from *Seinfeld*.

And I am married, so why does any of this matter?

Over the last month or so, my awareness of men has shifted in ways both uncomfortable and intriguing. An admiring male gaze is certainly not something I'm unaccustomed to. During my married years, I remained largely ambivalent about it, noting the attention only when it was unusually bold or in some way unavoidable. I had been claimed. I'd been forged in commitment emotionally and legally. There simply was no need to pay attention to whose eyes were on my ass.

I was occasionally aware of the subtle nod of approval from other men to my husband for his "catch," but it felt strange and odd. There is some secret male ritual that attributes special points to other men based on the attractiveness of the woman on their arm, as if it were an accomplishment to be rewarded. Not that I haven't heard plenty of women bestow equal admiration on others for "snaring" men of career accomplishment or wealth. And it, too, made my skin crawl. It is all vestiges of the Victorian concept of "marrying well" I assume. The modern equivalent of a dowry, perhaps. Or an outdated breeding ritual meant to ensure offspring would be suitably attractive and well-fed. But what am I to make of this dance as it plays out in my head? Do I want to leave my marriage? It feels like I'm testing the waters without wanting to get wet.

Yet suddenly, my gaze *is* on other men. My thoughts are, *What would it be like to date again?* Clearly, I have preconceived ideas that are neither flattering nor exciting about the potential candidates. And that doesn't delve into the fine-tuning of my requirement list. He can't be a smoker. Can't be a Trump Republican. Can't be someone who only eats frozen Hungry-Man meals or their equivalent. Yep, I'm a health-conscious, liberal Democrat, with a minor food-snob tendency, and I'm going to eat oysters and brussels sprouts in front of you. Men who consider dining at Olive Garden or TGI Fridays the pinnacle romantic experience need not apply.

Although I've agonized over living with my husband's history, I haven't lost my desire for him, yet my dreams are obsessively about a different man. I've been "well-tended to" during our relationship, to keep the Victorian euphemisms flowing. I suffer not from a lack of physical attention, passion, or orgasms. So what is it that I am craving?

From the start, my obsession was a schoolgirl crush with good sex dreams.

But a deeper issue is crying out, a deeper need lies buried underneath those lusty dreams. The obsession and the man at its source are a metaphor. A metaphor for something missing in my life and a mirror of what has been missing in me.

Those missing elements are clearer now. I can put names to them, although I suspect as time goes by, my understanding will deepen and layers I can't yet reach will emerge. This man has appeared in my dreams to teach me something.

What I now know is that I crave the touch of a man without memories of betrayal infiltrating the quiet moments in the afterglow of sex as passion settles into its soft, safe spot. What I crave is the attention of someone who looks at me with awe and anticipation for the things not yet revealed. For the discovery of the exact right spot on my neck to kiss that will make me gasp. For the spontaneous arm around my waist where I'm pulled in close just because the moment could not be resisted. What I crave is desire: the wanting, the anticipation, the need. What I crave is feeling those things unencumbered by betrayal. I crave the clarity and freedom of my own real and true emotions. I crave adoring a man the way I did through most of my marriage. I crave being adored in return.

I crave feeling true to myself, because my tragedy is that I have been walling off a segment of my heart, protecting it from being ravaged again. Trying not to allow it to die.

The true gift of my obsessive fantasy is that it has given me the opportunity to see not just possibility but how much I have lost of myself in the process of helping someone else heal. How much I have lost by trying to find a path forward while living with a pain that will not fade away. How much I have lost while smiling and nodding and dying inside.

I'm living a lesser life and have become a lesser version of myself than I ever realized.

That's what my obsession with men—well, one specific man—is really about. I can no longer face a future where dimmed happiness is a permanent state. I can no longer exist with partitioned emotions, endlessly hoping that someday, because we're doing the right things, I might again love with the full depth of my being. I can no longer subsist on hopes and wishes that now seem impossible to achieve. The dark cloud over our love is not leaving. The dark cloud that has become mine is not leaving.

My obsession has shown me that I've healed enough to feel, to want more. I've healed enough to recognize that I'm ready to live with my heart wide open once more, to risk, because the pain of staying is worse than an unknown future. But to do that I must leave.

CHAPTER FOURTEEN
TEARS ARE INVISIBLE IN THE SHOWER

As the day dawns, I remain wedged between sleep and wakefulness, unable to rouse myself fully, locked in the sexy escape that pulls at me, keeping me in that warm place. Eventually, the bright light of the sun intrudes through the bedroom curtains, forcing me into consciousness. I rise and step into the shower, still groggy after another night of disjointed sleep. My body moves slowly; my brain's still stuck in the honeyed dreams of my obsession. The sensation of his mouth trailing the back of my neck is still there, the feel of his fingers as they trace the ridges of my spine down the small of my back is still there. Real and lush. Steamy water cascades over my skin, forcing my mind into low gear, but I haven't shaken the heat of the dreams. The warmth is still fresh and intense and consuming.

I lift my head to the stream, wanting to hold on to the fantasy for a few minutes more. The glass door opens behind me, and my husband gives me a small smile, stepping in and reaching for the shampoo to wash my hair. Fantasy and reality collide. I close my eyes, feeling his hands massage my scalp, feeling his chest pressed against mine. Feeling the disconnection. I'm in another place still rich with the early morning dreams, but his hair is wrong, the heft of his shoulders is wrong, and I'm forced out of my fantasy.

I keep my eyes closed tight, unable to look at my husband, afraid he'll see everything I've hidden inside.

The tears come then. The tears of conflict and hurt and want. They glide down my face unnoticed, their saltiness mingling with the water. I cry for the loss of love, the loss of trust, for the wonderful parts of the relationship that can no longer be. I cry for the parts of my soul I've lost in the process. I cry for the love that remains in me but is no longer sustaining.

My back pressed against the slick, cool tile, I give in to the moment, letting my body respond to the unfulfilled desire. Sadness slowly shifts to passion until everything that is not us fades away and all I'm aware of is his mouth, his hands, and our collective heat.

Later, as I towel off and comb through damp strands of hair, I see anew the conflict in my eyes. I see the love. Or is it a moment of regret? Regret for what should have been, what was supposed to be. Regret for what he destroyed so carelessly.

I stare in the mirror at eyes hollow and unfamiliar. Rivulets of water trickle down the side of my neck, trailing over skin now warm and pink. With legs still rubbery and a pulse only beginning its decline, I look at my reflection, startled by the emptiness in my face.

What have I become? Who have I become? The thoughts bounce around unanswerable. Even when I reach for him, even when my mouth finds his, even when my body shudders and trembles with release, there is a part of me untouched, untouchable.

Buried deep inside is something frozen and hidden. Something surrounded by a protective mantle insulating me from further pain. It is so deep and so solidly formed I've been unaware of its existence, and now, like an archaeological dig, the shadow of its shape pokes through, calling me to uncover it. Now revealed, its existence will not be denied.

It's that piece of my heart capable of full abandonment. It's the piece of my heart that I've held on to, sheltered away rather than given fully for fear of one last fatal blow.

It's the piece of my heart that I give generously only in my obsessive dreams. There, in my fantasies, I can live and love with abandon once again. It's the place where I no longer have to protect my fragile heart. The place where tenderness and passion and trust can again exist.

All of this I see in that moment, hidden deep behind my hollow eyes. I'm aware of its existence. Aware of its source. And aware that I no longer want to live empty and hollow and protecting my heart. I no longer want to live diminished.

CHAPTER FIFTEEN
DECISIONS

Cold air blows against my bare legs as I struggle to adjust the position of my feet in the stirrups. The paper cloth covering my naked lower half is a poor insulator against the air conditioning. What inhumane fool decided it was a good idea for women to lie flat on our backs on an exam table, naked, and spread for interminable amounts of time waiting for a doctor to arrive? Bonus points if you're meeting the doctor for the first time in this position. It sure wasn't a chick.

Tears well up, sliding down my cheeks and into my hair, and I wipe them away with the back of my hand. I lift my head and see a box of tissues on a shelf across the room. I debate extracting myself from the torture device long enough to grab a wad, calculating that the minute my bare backside is off the table the door will open.

I imagine I'm not the first woman to break down in the middle of her annual pelvic exam. In fact, the memory of a similar sniffly episode comes back: a moment shortly after I learned of my husband's infidelities and I needed confirmation that he hadn't compromised my physical health in addition to my mental health.

And here I am again. In the strange synchronistic ways of the universe, the circle completes. One teary gynecologic exam at the start, another as I make the decision to leave him.

I wipe my damp cheeks, and the exam proceeds without issue. But the irony of the timing doesn't leave me. I carry it with me as I run errands, working through the task list that is part of snowbird life. We'll be returning to Florida in a few days and there are items to pack, things to ship, mail forwarding to arrange.

And now an attorney to secure.

Later, as I stand in line at the post office with an armful of boxed, signed novels ready to ship, hot tears slide under my mask. I stare at a stain in the acoustic tile on the dropped ceiling hoping that focusing on something stupid will distract me, taking deep, slow breaths and wiping my wet eyes with the back of my hand for the second time that day.

I've been in line only minutes, but knowing definitively I'm going to end my marriage, a realization slams into my head. I've forgiven my husband. Finally, I can say it with complete honesty, something I had never been able to say before. Not to myself and not to him.

Will letting go of the anger help hold me together when the dark moments and loneliness descend on me in the months to come?

I pay for my shipping and turn to leave, maneuvering through the halls back toward the street, when another thought stops me. This, the need to end the marriage, is about forgiving myself for having stayed. Forgiving myself for what has felt like a lack of courage. Forgiving myself for loving so deeply that I believed I could live with anything as long as I was loved in return and we were trying together to make it right.

The therapist's question, the one with her prescription pad at the ready, came back into my head. "Is love enough?" she had asked.

It turns out the answer to that question is no; no it isn't enough. It isn't enough for me, although it's taken so very long for me to know that with certainty. It isn't enough when that love has left me feeling broken and empty. It isn't enough when I'd wondered if I'd always feel alone and crushed even in the midst of a marriage.

It isn't enough when my self-worth is on the line.

I've struggled with this long enough to know that my fear of leaving has been, in part, the fear of being alone. Fear that my introverted tendencies would leave me in my apartment with no one to talk to but my cat for days on end. Would leave me sitting in front of the TV, night after night, watching pretend lives play out rather than living one of my own. Would leave me alone in my bed, night after night, without a man's kiss or caress or a strong shoulder to lie on.

I realized today, standing there in the post office, that those fears would only be true if I let them. Only by setting aside the pain and emptiness, only by forging a new life, only by saying goodbye could I open a place for all the love I have to give to find a new and proper home. Only by saying goodbye would there be the possibility that I would receive in turn what I have given out.

Rather profound for a ten-minute stop at a one-person post office buried in the lower level of the Hancock Building, but the universe apparently doesn't give a shit where you are or when. Knowing strikes when it strikes. Listen to the universe or miss its message.

Will this decision hold? It feels like it this time. Clarity. Another gift delivered, wrapped in a pretty bow by my obsession.

I mentally tumble through the logistics. When will I tell him? What will I say? What will I say to the kids? What is the work ahead of me when it comes to housing and financial decisions?

I wander our apartment, room to room, ostensibly preparing for our migration south, awash in memories. My hand glides over the soft boucle of the midcentury chair I had reupholstered. I adjust the position of ceramic vases I picked up at an art show in San Francisco. I run my eyes around the condo I renovated, taking in each detail. Floating between worlds. Memories of our boys preparing dinner on Mother's Day, Father's Day, and birthdays come back. I look at the dining table and can see the four of us together, can hear the boys planning the menu and laughing as they made a terrible mess. I remember our blind, incontinent cocker spaniel, Bailey, as he bumped around in his diaper, perpetually following my husband by scent. There are memories of standing at the window, arms around each other in the dark on Saturday nights, watching the fireworks on Navy Pier.

Life on pause stretches in front of me with no end or plan for whatever comes next. I want to stay in the happy past and skip over the uncertainty of what this decision might bring. But as I tentatively step forward in my life, it seems I should analyze the reticence that has held me hostage. Has it been love alone? Obligation? The knowledge of everything my husband has done to try to keep me in his life? Or has it simply been fear?

I want to believe it's been love that held me, but I suspect fear has weighed in heavily. There is fear of the divorce process: the ugliness of it as attorneys push for a win. Fear that the details of my husband's behavior would need to be torn apart and rehashed all over again. Fear that, in that process, I would learn the rest. I've never believed I've known everything he's done, so there would likely be a question or slip-up or something to bring the emotional pain of betrayal crashing down on me again as another old lie surfaced. Fear that, through the process, anger or ego would push us both to a place where the need to win or to hold on to a moment of internal strength would find us inflicting even more pain on each other.

In more ways than I want to admit, fear has kept me chained. Maybe *restricted* is a better word. It's been a leash keeping me within the boundaries of my existing life. But why did I choose it?

Divorce is ultimately about power—who has it, who has the more aggressive attorney, and who is willing to fight to the death no matter the emotional cost. Regardless of the reasons for divorce, and who filed, stereotypes prevail. Men fight with the one tool they consistently seem to possess: the urge to win. And with the legal process largely about dividing assets, winning for men is about getting a bigger share of the dollars. Emotional wreckage, theirs or their partner's, doesn't matter.

Women hold back in the fight because the reality of emotional wreckage is already front and center in our lives. We acquiesce when we shouldn't, give up too much to get too little, all for the sake of our emotional health. Men don't seem to share that burden. It occurs to me that perhaps compartmentalization plays a part here as well. Perhaps the emotional toll hits them after the ink is dry, the money has been transferred, and they're faced with sitting alone in a sparsely furnished rental, a microwaved dinner on the coffee table in front of them, wondering who is going to scrub the damn toilet. Then men finally replace the anger they had used as a coping mechanism with loneliness.

Many of the women I know who've been in this awful place were lonely in their marriages long before that first consultation with a divorce attorney.

As was I. I was lonely when I was the sober one not drowning my sorrows in vodka. Lonely when I felt my efforts at saving him were useless. Yet most of us stay for far too long or past the point where compromise had any pretext of equality. We stay because of financial fear. We stay because of the children. We stay because a lonely marriage seems an insufficient reason to unravel our lives. We stay because the thought of the ugliness of the divorce process is too much. We stay because we can't picture life on the other side. We stay because change is really, really, really hard.

We stay until the pain we feel while staying is worse than what we imagine the pain of leaving will be.

Now, the pressure to take a step forward sits in my chest impossible to ignore. Again, I feel like a fraud. I crawl into bed each night as if nothing has changed inside me and look at him asleep next to me, regret tugging at my heart, before I tiptoe out of bed in the middle of the night, my tears falling again and again for what should have been. I hold back and hide my truth some more, keeping my silence in a marriage I know I'm going to leave in a few weeks. Will I also stock up on groceries and make sure the laundry is done on my way out the door so he won't have to?

Strangely, anger and irritation are also right under the surface. Nothing new or anger-inducing has happened. I'm angry with myself—even though I shouldn't be—for allowing the indecision to add to my grief. I try to tell myself that this was happening only because I was emotionally ready for it to happen. Underneath, I know that had we ended the marriage when I learned of his infidelity, there would have been a reconciliation. There was still too much love. Damaged, flawed love, but love nonetheless. When the time comes in the next few weeks for "the conversation," I know he will ask if I still love him. And my answer will be yes, but I need to leave anyway. I can't exist broken like this any longer.

I'm already playing out what to say, how to say it, and prepping for his likely responses. They're the mental practice runs that I inevitably do before tough conversations. I'm afraid of the words. Afraid of the finality. Afraid, in saying it, I will acquiesce when I hear the tug of love and our history in my own voice.

Is he anticipating this? He said so once, said he thought there would come a point where his history would be too weighty for me to live with. Perhaps too much time has transpired and he's set those thoughts aside. We've had conversations recently about my sadness, but I've changed my mind so many times—I've walked out and left for a few days while I tried to sort through emotions only to come back—that leaving itself has gotten old, even to me.

But this time, it's not the quagmire of pain and indecision and questions of "How could he?" I know what I want to do. No, that's not quite right. I don't *want* this. This is what I *need* to do for myself and my future.

Life comes at us in small moments.

Looking back—when we allow ourselves or are forced to—changes the movie of our lives. We can, if we work hard, see the culmination of the events that shape us. But it takes work. We must make it happen. Avoiding the themes that we see there, the ones that hurt us, will keep the hurt in a place where it can still do harm.

Pain lives deepest in avoidance.

We don't recognize it that way. We avoid facing reality, falsely believing we are protecting ourselves, but avoidance simply makes the pain more insidious, more damaging. Avoidance and inaction cement it to our psyche, turning hurt into a leech, draining us of vitality until we have become someone else. Until we've become a thing we don't recognize.

I fought for my husband's sobriety—for his life—for most of our years together. Now it's time to fight for my own.

A small suitcase sits tucked next to the credenza in my office. In it are financial documents, bank information, my passport—the business essentials of life. No sense in unpacking them now. It's become a "go bag" waiting for the moment I will walk out of my marriage.

As we settle back into our life in Florida, I catch myself thinking that nothing has changed at least five times a day, that I'm not moments away from starting divorce proceedings and leaving my husband. It would be so easy to set aside the decision because, at the moment, life seems fine. There is no fighting, no stony silence, no glaring looks, no tears threatening to spill. Life is normal, whatever that means.

We stock the fridge with produce from the drive-through farmer's market. We cook our meals together. My husband shares stories about the latest business dramas in his work life. I tell him about a conversation I had with a guy who wants advice on how to get a publisher interested in his book when he hasn't written more than a list of events and still believes a sale should be imminent. We laugh at the cat's latest antics and grumble endlessly in joint outrage over the latest political charade on the nightly news.

In the past, it was this normalcy that would have pushed thoughts of divorce to the recesses of my mind. *This is just a phase*, I would tell myself. Those thoughts come and go occasionally. How could they not after all I've been through? But this is also the thinking that kept me seesawing emotionally, blinded to my own empty heart. It's the thinking that allowed a fantasy obsession to consume me.

As this routine settles in and questions such as "Should I?" and "Is this really the right thing?" flit around the edges of my mind, I'm again aware of the pull of maintaining the status quo, aware that I still feel love but, surprisingly, am not paralyzed by it like I've been in the past. The fear is waning. At least the fear of what might come if I leave him. The fear of being alone.

The stronger pull is the fear that if I stay, I'll be imprisoning myself in a half-dead life, where I remain silent, numb, unfeeling, and empty. I will become that mechanical Stepford wife with only a plastic toy heart inside my chest.

Days before we traveled south, I had lunch with my friend Stacy—a minor act of rebellious normalcy in an otherwise not-normal world. Our conversations are always deep, complex, and heartfelt. It didn't take long before I told her everything: my decision to end my marriage, how it came about, and why now.

She knew enough about my marital history to not be terribly surprised. "You look at peace," she said. There was no judgment, no worry for me, no questioning whether I had fully considered the gravity of the decision. Instead, we spoke about the underlying emotional tug of long-lasting love, the ways in which women find their truth or grow into themselves in the middle stage of our lives. We spoke of identity, responsibility, and self-respect. In other words, just an average lunch for two women when the foundation has collapsed under their feet.

I recognized the contentment as it washed over me while I told my tale. It wasn't joy for the end of a marriage but resolve. I adored this man, a man I had loved with every ounce of my being, and it was breaking my heart all over again to know that I needed to leave.

This time in our lives, after sobriety was secured, was to be our time, a new honeymoon stage, I had thought. Instead, I'm coming back to my own truth, my own power, making a decision for me, finally, after a lifetime of putting others first. I'm putting my own survival front and center. As dramatic as that may sound, it is about survival. Survival of my psyche, my ability to feel happiness, and my self-respect.

What I was feeling was release.

Until that lunch, until I said it all out loud, I hadn't fully realized how the pain of betrayal had eaten away at my self-respect. How the pain of those years fighting for his sobriety had drained me. I drove home from our lunch in the suburbs feeling at peace for the first time in as long as I could remember.

Now, as I sit in this holding pattern, as the anxiety about making my announcement creeps in, I wander my condo thinking again about logistics. Will he want to stay here? Will we sell it? Where will I go?

To clear my head, I walk along the water past the newly opened pier, watching happy faces, and transport myself back to that lunch and invite back the calm certainty, pushing the anxiety away. I reexperience the wash of contentment. The knowing smile I felt on my face told me I was not only doing the right thing but the necessary thing, and I was doing it because it was what was needed.

It is what I have to do.

My life depends on it.

Little by little, day by day, each time I wasn't true to myself, a few more cells of my heart died, constricting my capacity for love. After years of too much pain and trying so hard to hold on to something that was important to me, I couldn't see I had become a shell of myself.

The illusions are gone now, as is the indecision. Gone without animosity. Gone without anger. Will my heart and my self-respect regenerate?

A quote from Joseph Campbell appeared in my Facebook feed this morning in an ad for my friend Ann's talisman jewelry. "We must be willing to get rid of the life we planned, so as to have the life that is waiting for us." The universe was sending me a well-timed message it seems. As today is the day I will end my marriage.

Sometimes I think he'll be expecting this, perhaps has been expecting this all along, knowing that he would never have chosen to stay if I had been the one to discard him. At other times, I think he'll be stunned. So wrapped in the agony of this decision, still loving him, still broken and hurt and betrayed, I can't tell what I perceive is true and objective anymore. I only know I can't go on like this.

I am dying. Slowly, one molecule at a time.

Shaking, I interrupt him in his office late in the afternoon. He's at his desk, computer open. I sit in the chair across from him, my hands balled into fists, my nails digging into my flesh because the effort keeps me from turning around and walking out. It keeps me from changing my mind, continuing the cycle of indecision that has become an unfair agony of its own.

"I can't do this anymore," I say.

"Do what?" he asks, his face registering the pain he sees in mine. I can see in his eyes what he fears I'm about to say, but he needs me to say out loud. I can see the tightness in his body as he anticipates the gut punch.

"Be married," I say, the words barely loud enough for me to hear as my throat clenches and the tears cascade.

His head drops for a moment. He closes his eyes and pinches the bridge of his nose the way he does when the news is too tough for a response.

"Does this have anything to do with COVID?"

"In part," I mumble. "It's shown me I can't live the rest of my life this empty." There is too much in that question for a more thorough response. Too many words underneath the words. And COVID is the accelerator, not the disease.

"You don't love me anymore?"

"I can't live with your past."

"Is there anything I can do to change your mind?"

"No."

He wants the fix, the "if I do X, she'll still love me. She'll stay." He's wanted it all along, we both did. But the sutures we've applied can't cover the angry gash that has left my heart and my love and my self-respect infected.

He stares across the room, unable to look at my face. He hangs his head. His voice is choked when he says to himself, "I'm going to die alone."

There is nothing else for either of us to say, nothing that hasn't been said or promised or screamed or fought about or cried about ad nauseam. Not that history stops my tears or my sorrow.

I've broken his heart, and what's left of mine crumbles like dust as I walk out of his office, blinded by my own hurt.

I stumble into our bedroom, let out one big sob as I choke back tears, my body heaving. I slip off my wedding ring and put it in my jewelry drawer, trying to pretend it's just another pretty piece of metal. Afraid that I'll change my mind, I stand in our closet and quickly begin to pack. I hear him come in, and he tells me I don't need to leave right away. There are appointments on the calendar. "Wait a few days," he says.

Nearly suffocating with tears, I say, "Thank you." I can't look at him. It's official.

Numb, we fumble through the rest of the evening, managing dinner together where we push food around on a plate, eating little, tasting nothing, saying nothing. A box of tissues sits on the table next to my glass because the tears won't stop. I eye the bottle of wine on the kitchen counter and wonder if I should forgo the glass and just finish the damn thing in one sitting. Anything to blunt this pain. The pain I've inflicted on him and on myself.

He takes the guest room, leaving me alone behind a closed door in our bed. I'm as lonely as I was after I'd asked him to leave years earlier.

Propping myself up with pillows, I try to distract myself with a stupid movie that doesn't hold my interest; I simply need the sound of voices in the room. I fight the urge to curl up into that ball I'd been in back then, the one that kept me frozen.

I listen to the sounds at the end of the hall that now seems miles long, wondering how he's doing, wondering if he'll come into our room in the middle of the night to try to change my mind one last time, wondering if he, too, feels the need to be held. Even with this pain, I long for him to comfort me. Long to bury myself in his chest and to feel his arms around me as I sob. That's been his role for nearly twenty-five years. He's the person I turn to when an embrace is the only salve that could take away the pain, even when the pain was something that he had caused. But walking down the hall to his room wouldn't help either of us. There is no "and both" in this equation.

There is no one who can comfort me tonight.

The conflict wrenches me open all over again, confusing me. There will be no sleep tonight or likely the night after. How can I have the desire to be held and comforted by the very person who has caused me so much pain? How can I love someone who has caused so much agony without regard for my welfare? I don't know how to separate his role as the man who loved me, my comforter-in-chief, and my husband from the man who tore me apart. I don't know how to set aside our history, the good parts of our love.

My heart is a bloody pile of debris. There is still love, and there is still affection. Twenty-five years can't be erased. Will time heal all wounds? Time wasn't enough to heal the hurt of betrayal. Will it heal the hurt of leaving?

This is so hard. So damn ugly hard. Emotions bombard me like a hailstorm, pelting me with icy reality. I'm leaving a man I still love. I'm leaving a man I know loves me.

I've held my resolve even as I look at his eyes, empty with sorrow, while his body deflated. The dark pit inside me grows with the pain I am now causing. Tears are near the surface night and day. I sit in my office trying to write, trying to avoid seeing his pain, but my eyes are so irritated and swollen I can no longer see my computer screen. Instead, I stare blankly out the window at nothing, not knowing what to do with myself. We're existing in this place of shock. In separate bedrooms. Eating meals together. Conversation is limited but cordial as we begin to separate ourselves from each other. I feel like a robot, shutting down, afraid to touch the emotions raging in me for fear of collapse. Sometimes I'm overcome with the profound sadness of it all and ball myself up in my bed and let the tears do what they must.

History, moments, parts of our past flood my mind. Things said, things done, things left unsaid.

The question that haunts me, the question I long to ask is, "Were they all worth it? Was it all worth the agony you've inflicted on us?" But I don't ask. I've dished out enough guilt-inducing language over the years that it would serve no useful purpose now, yet it's on my mind. They are questions that have never been answered, can't be answered until he is alone and forced to deal with his own loneliness, I suspect. I don't know if those questions haunted him during our previous separation the way they've haunted me. I can only deal with my own grief now.

But will this new hit threaten his sobriety, bring new vulnerability for relapse? Is that my responsibility too? I think not. I've done what I can, but the sadness and regret for where we are is overwhelming, nonetheless.

I pack the balance of the financial documents I'll need. I assemble the research materials for my latest manuscript, as if, miraculously, I'll be able to focus. But the uncertainty of the next six months is hard to work through. How long will I stay in Florida? How difficult will it be to sell our property? Where do I store things, and what the hell will I need in my new life, whatever that looks like? Will the legal process shred me further?

Feeling like a caged animal with nowhere to go, I pace, sort through clothes as if it matters, looking for that safe lair, but there is none. I'm moving into the vulnerability where I have no home, utterly unsure of when I will feel grounded again, unsure of when I will feel safe again. Without a firm picture of where and how I'll live, I'm unmoored. So I resort to the one thing I can do right now: make a damn list. I need to get these logistical, tactical thoughts out of my head and onto paper to be ticked off. I'm good at that. The to-do list.

What do I do with my mail? Will my cat be overly stressed? How many book boxes will I need? Will the legal process grind to a halt if I leave the state and go back to Chicago? What season of clothing do I keep handy? What do I put in storage? What do I do with my painting studio? Did I stop the wine delivery?

Important stuff, that. For now, it's all I have.

———————

It's time to face the world. I've held off on the phone calls to the kids, my dad, and my friends. Whether I was afraid I'd change my mind or just needed to be someplace that felt safe to talk, I'm not sure.

With COVID raging, I've packed what I think I'll need for a couple of months and driven south from our condo in St. Petersburg to the Naples property we had been renting out until COVID chased away the seasonal renters. It won't make me feel settled to stay here, but it's the practical choice while the limbo of the legal process and longer-term decisions play out.

Privilege allows me the option of an easy place to live. My decision about my marriage wasn't based on harsh financial realities of what "after" would look like. Privilege eases the tactical impact of divorce, but no amount of money eases the emotional pain.

In Naples, mask-less individuals roam my building and wander grocery stores and businesses unconcerned about everyone around them. I contact the building manager to ask about the mask policy. Her reply? "We don't have one." My stay here will be in a beautiful isolation ward, but I'm grateful I have a place to go. St. Pete, as it's known, wasn't perfect, but here, COVID denial is rampant. Increasingly, I'm angry with the selfishness I see around me, and it's magnified by the selfishness of my husband that brought me here.

I start my calls with my father and then my boys. Shock and confusion are the response. "What happened?" my dad asks, convinced, of course, that some new hurt must have been inflicted on me.

Choked with tears, I simply tell him, "No, nothing new. I just can't live with his past."

Confusion sits in the "Hmmm" I get in response. That's his version of empathy and probing support. It isn't that he lacks empathy, he's just of that generation where don't ask, don't tell applied to all of life's emotional challenges, not only sexual orientation.

The kids are more direct, expressing the need to sit with the news a little longer, understanding that processing comes in waves. The youngest asks how I am and if he can do anything for me. The older— more internal in his emotions—says little.

Given our previous separation, this announcement, although surprising, was not out of left field. Yet it stung.

"But you seemed so happy," was the common thread from those who didn't know the truth of our history. From those that knew the small pieces came quiet understanding. Before I departed for Naples, I asked my husband what he'd like to say when asked by those who would expect an explanation for our divorce. It felt important to offer a graceful, coordinated exit story. His response was, "We couldn't work through our past conflict."

I looked at him, stunned, but didn't argue. He hadn't presented our "past conflict" in a truthful light, and his response now was one that offered no hint of blame or responsibility. Instead, he wanted to spin this as some vague mutual decision born of mutual consideration. But we weren't two people who simply fell out of love or had a rough patch. There is blame here, and I'm irritated, feeling the need for vindication, perhaps. Or feeling the need for public acknowledgment that he treated me badly, that he feels regret for what he did.

I know regret is there, but he can't admit what he did or admit the reality of who he was to others, and his silence now grates like his silence of the past. The private man and the public man are not the same in his mind; he's hidden it all from even those closest to him. And that hurts all over again.

Despite my desire for a coordinated response, I can't follow his lead and perpetuate the lies any longer.

CHAPTER SIXTEEN
SHREDDING

Routine, such that it is, has started to settle in. A faux reality carries me through the day. I write, badly. I walk on the beach in the early morning when the weather suits, hoping the salt air will cleanse my head and my heart. It's difficult to hold on to rage or emptiness when waves are crashing and seagulls poke urgently at prey buried in the sand. Back in the apartment, my latest novel pushes me away until guilt forces a few hundred poorly conceived words to form.

The document-gathering stage of divorce has begun. Twelve months of statements for this account, three months for that one, titles, deeds, copies for me, him, attorneys, the court. I trudge to the copy center and, nearly two hours later, emerge with fifteen piles of folders, clipped and organized. My share of the documents alone will probably top five hundred pages. It seems silly, but the court is not a flexible entity, so I dig and print and crunch and start a spreadsheet that will form the shell of our financial negotiations.

Weeks have passed since the anger I felt over my husband's behavior last clutched at my chest, but as I sit alone in an apartment I don't want to be in—an apartment that had been our home during the worst of our marriage—contemplating my future, my thoughts swing and the knife in my heart that has been present for far too long and embedded far too deep twists again.

I look around the condo, trying to remember the promise this apartment was supposed to hold for us when we bought it. I look out at the crashing waves, the sandy beach, the stunning sunsets, and can't recall a single fond memory. I hate it here. Betrayal and hurt ooze from the walls, having never been exorcised, just like they ooze from my heart. Each day, I'm forced to revisit the place where I lay curled on the floor. Each day, I'm forced to revisit the phantom of the worst of my marriage.

How many tears must I shed before I can heal? A bucket full? A bathtub? A river? An ocean? Someone needs to tell me so I know when this hurt will be gone.

And what does healing from all of this look like? Is it a feeling? A realization that some random detail or memory or word choice that would have triggered anger or anxiety no longer does? A Lifetime movie where, one day in the near future, I float barefoot over the beach, sun glinting off my hair, my skin a pale golden glow, and a serene, contented smile on my face?

Will I simply wake up one day feeling lighter and hopeful in a way I haven't for longer than I can remember? Or will this be a slow dawning awareness that what should have been no longer enters my mind?

Or will I only know I've healed if I can again trust another man with my heart?

It feels important to know, as if there should be some doctor's note or certificate of completion that I can be awarded that officially ends my mourning. But I can't yet conceive of the benchmark that will signal "all clear." Maybe it doesn't work that way.

Perhaps I should simply think of healing as something that comes in layers or stages. It seems fitting. The AA model of a twelve-step program adapted for another use.

If my healing, this grief, is a twelve-step program, what would that look like? Where would I be in the journey, like those in that world like to call it?

Step one: admit I had become powerless, and life had become unmanageable. Check.

Step two: make a searching and fearless moral inventory of ourselves. Fearless, hmm. Still working on that one.

Step three: humbly ask Him to remove our shortcomings. This is farther down the list, which is encouraging, but it doesn't match my views of God. That one needs reworking. And what does *shortcomings* mean? The fact that I stayed? Which of my shortcomings needs to be addressed? Was I too trusting? Too loving? Should I have dumped him earlier? Was my failing that I assumed when this man professed his love and adoration for me that he meant it in the same way I did?

This is the hard one. It's the single thing that I've never been able to wrap into a neat, concise explanation to be trotted out on demand.

Me. Why did I stay as long as I stayed after I knew my husband had disrespected me so thoroughly?

I suspect that question alone isn't even the right question, although I ask it. I lack another way to wrap it into a neat package. It's a question asked by others who didn't live the agony or the love, nor understand how much I truly adored this man. Others who didn't understand what it feels like to believe, accurately or not, that I was the only thing standing between the person I loved and his death. How do I explain the need to save a loved one from self-destruction? That to walk away is to leave them alone in that fight, without tools or clarity or a safe place to land.

How do I explain that his behavior, even the ugliest of it, was never about me? It was his damaged heart. It was the hole inside him that he was filling, his unspoken belief that he was not deserving of love. Not deserving of *my* love.

The lies he told himself were even more insidious than the lies he told me.

I was just collateral damage.

Underneath the pain and the psychological morass, these questions are about what I was willing to do for love. And what it takes for love to die. The deepest of loves only dies a slow and tortured death regardless of how the final blow was dealt. Its foundation is so entwined with who we are and what we've been, that part of us must be cut away, amputated, if we hope to save the rest.

I thought I'd taken the sharp knife and pruned the roots of the disease that was choking me of life, but it seems now that I'm still in that shallow plastic pot waiting to be replanted, waiting for a new place to grow strong. I water and fertilize what I can inside myself to build strength and resolve.

But the conflict that roils me still as I probe the confusing layers of what has been is about something else. It's about me. Why was I willing to go down too? To throw myself on the sacrificial fire of his destruction? I did not see my own life draining away like a deep slice in my skin that would not clot. I was bleeding out faster than my body could rebuild red blood cells. I took no notice. I built no support. I kept the damage quiet, sharing only those snippets I could contain within a scripted storyline with those who loved me.

Why? It feels weak as I look back on it from a distance, yet I know the parts that were strong.

I was strong for him but could not be strong for myself. I could advocate and nudge and plead for his salvation, but not for my own.

For that, I have no answer. For that, I have not found peace. Perhaps that is where my healing lies.

I struggle and push emotions aside, trying to focus on the tasks at hand. The business of divorce is vast and time-consuming. But at night, alone in bed, I drift back to my lifeline. I revisit my obsession. I dream of a time, some point in the distance, where I might again be capable of love. Where I might again feel the longing and desire and optimism present in my fantasies. I dream of tenderness and passion. I dream of a place, a time, where I can trust again.

Can I get to that place, or will the loneliness swallow me? Am I forever damaged? Forever unable to trust?

A woman with her heart bound.

I'm existing. I'm doing. I'm taking the tiny baby steps to move forward and fighting to suppress anxiety about the uncertainty of my life.

Just as driving through the country in the dark, one can only see what is illuminated by the headlights. Yet foot by foot, mile by mile, the journey progresses.

————————

My phone rings. It's my father.

"I thought maybe you could come up to the lake and take care of me this winter. Since you're single now." As it often is, his tone is jokey, teasing, but he is a man who couches his ask.

"I don't think I have adequate gear to get through a Wisconsin winter," I shoot back, laughing. I try to pretend his words weren't code for a well-thought-through request.

He needs help. He's done the unthinkable and asked. It isn't his nature by personality or generation to admit there is anything he can't manage. So he turns to me, not my coupled siblings who live in the same state. After all, what else would I, a self-employed, soon-to-be divorced woman do with herself during COVID lockdown? It sure as hell isn't dating.

The minute I hear those words, I know his health is worse than he'd let on. I remain noncommittal on the phone, but know I would be there.

We hang up, and I immediately call my sister, asking for her assessment. She already had plans to see him over the weekend.

"Do you need help?" she asked him a few days later.

"It wouldn't hurt," he responded.

It was as close to begging as the man was capable of.

I repack the items I thought I would need for a Florida winter, boxing the warm-weather clothes for storage, regrouping on work materials, books, personal items. I prep for a new version of winter.

The "lick my wound with long beach walks" healing I had imagined is set aside. Instead, I ponder whether taking on the role of caregiver will prolong my own emotional instability or help ease the transition to a life alone? The thought is selfish and uncomfortable, yet the ask is a stark reminder of how often my life has involved suppression of my needs for the sake of others.

I, of course, can't say no. I would never refuse a request of this nature from my father.

The SUV is packed. I drive back to St. Pete having no regrets about leaving a place that magnifies my loneliness but worried and confused about how this necessary shift will affect my emotions. Uncertain of how time will play out, I unload boxes at my art studio for storage. Running my eyes over the tall ceilings, the open space, the well-placed lighting, I stack bins in the corner. An unfinished canvas tacked to the wall cries out for a dash of yellow ochre, but I suppress the urge and leave my brushes untouched in the tall white crock holding them, wondering how long it will be until I can again find solace in my creative urges. This beautiful healing space will now sit unused, serving instead as an expensive holding place for dreams. Another part of me I must set aside.

My husband and I meet for lunch. We sit across the table from each other on the outdoor patio at one of our favorite restaurant haunts—the taquitos and salsa are a thick hedge between us—afraid to look in each other's eyes, our voices flat and hesitant. Emotion sits just below the surface as we discuss the logistics of listing our condo for sale. With the change of plans and knowing I may not be returning to Florida before it sells, there is an urgency to the work. We are strangers now, two people who share a history needing to use the language of business to communicate lest emotion crushes us.

The food has no taste; the background music, no melody. The weight of our estrangement numbs us to everything but our regret.

Returning to our condo, I swap the summer clothes in my suitcase for winter, shuffle through paperwork for any last-minute essentials I may need, and hide in the bathroom to cry.

"It didn't have to be like this," I silently wail. Unanswered questions haunt me still. *If he could betray me so easily, did he ever love me?* It's one of those damn questions asked and answered a million times already. Yet regardless of how profusely or how often he has professed his love, the reality of his actions has not allowed me to accept that completely as truth. I don't share his skill at compartmentalization. I can't understand his "yes, but . . ." behavior. I can't view love that way.

Despite my insecurity, underneath it all, I believe he did love me, and still does. The only way to process the disconnection is to conclude that he loved me in the only way he is capable of. Clearly, I've lived these many years feeling and believing I was loved. I couldn't have stayed the last few years with a man I believed was lying about the core emotion at the heart of marriage. But these moments of vulnerability slam me up against the wall, and the false reality won't let go.

My brain tells me it was himself he didn't love. My heart has other questions. It's the contradiction I'll need to make peace with.

Falling back into old patterns, even in this current false reality, we prepare dinner together, returning to the habit that had been our routine. He prepares the entrée; I, the vegetable. We chop and stir in silence, and I give him a wide berth—afraid of accidentally touching, I suppose. Afraid that, if I do, I won't be able to let go.

We sit on opposite ends of the dining table like strangers to keep COVID precautions in place. I suppose it's fitting. Everything about this is foreign. I look at him and see the gauntness in his cheeks, the dark circles under his eyes, and all I can feel is the vice crushing my heart.

Our meal finished, he wants to talk. I can tell he's been planning this, waiting for the right moment. I notice his wedding ring is finally off, and it catches me off guard. Stabs at me. It shouldn't, but it does. And the tears start all over again. He tells me he hopes I will let him check in with me and hopes I will do the same. He wants me to know that I can lean on him when it gets tough to be up north with my dad. He's there if I need someone to talk to.

He's worried about me walking into another COVID-denial environment. Worried that I'm compromising my own emotional healing by caring for another in a place that will repel me.

His words are raw and painful, full of regret.

"You've given me a gift these last few years, one I didn't deserve," he says, choking on the words. "I shouldn't feel this way, since I'm the one who did this."

I keep my eyes glued to the shadow my wine glass makes on the table as I cry. I have no response. I can't meet his eyes. I can't make him feel better anymore. Can't tell him it's okay, that he will be okay. I've done that work for years. I can only sit with my own pain. But I feel some relief, vindication perhaps, that he accepts his role in the pain he's inflicted on me.

A nagging disconnect and shock seem to sit under the surface of his words as if he never expected this day would come, as if the depth of his pain is catching him by surprise.

Tears still constrict my throat, silencing me.

Who will tell me I will be okay?

"I'm fine," he says. "Do what you need to. Get here when you can."

My father insists that his need for help is not urgent. I'm hesitant, listening for any doubt in his voice, knowing his penchant for minimizing his own obstacles, but the Chicago condo also needs to be put up for sale. There is prep work to be done. I need winter clothes, a car, snow tires.

With COVID raging, I've loaded hand sanitizer in my purse, double masked, braved a flight, and returned to Chicago to spend a couple of days preparing our apartment for sale and myself for winter in the snow, something I'd hoped to never experience again.

I wander our apartment trying to view it through the eyes of a buyer. Trying to separate the personal from the practical. Trying to think financially, not emotionally. I declutter, box family photos, and rearrange art I've been meaning to adjust for five years. I finally buy that rug the dining room has been screaming for.

It's the work of ending a marriage.

Each drawer I open, each shelf I clean off, each closet I clear of extraneous clothes for the Salvation Army, is a moment of our life together. It's a memory of a family, a memory of love.

It's memories of a night my husband abruptly dropped the phone when our cat decided she was auditioning for the Flying Wallendas—walking the four-inch window ledge outside our kitchen, thirteen floors above the street—while I tried to decipher what I was hearing on the other end of the call. Watching the acrobatics of the Blue Angels during the August Air Show from our balcony. Our youngest bringing eight friends home from college on sporadic weekends, parking kids on anything resembling a bed. Each tiny memory is precious; each one crushes me again.

With the realtor lined up, boxes I haven't looked at in years need to be assessed for storage or the trash. I find an unmarked manila envelope. Inside are dozens of cards—love notes, birthday cards—from my husband. I look away, close my eyes, toss the lot into the trash, and sink to my knees, the tears collapsing me.

I thought I was stronger. I thought I had perspective. But once again, every moment of our life together is back in question. What, if anything, was real? Was each and every tender memory something I alone experienced while my husband was preoccupied with covering his lies?

I don't want to be angry anymore, but here in our home, preparing it for someone else to cherish, the anger resurfaces. At this moment, it feels like I've never let it escape, never lost control. That rage is still rotting inside me.

I clean, pack, and shove the anger back down into my gut, trying to imagine a life that I can't yet see. The immediate task list is long, and it helps to have things to do, but already I'm anxious to picture what might be in front of me, both with my dad's health and with my own life. I want a marker on the calendar for when my new life will begin.

The evening before I'm to drive the six hours to northern Wisconsin, I sit with a large glass of cabernet beside me, a shredder at my feet, and the TV turned to the evening political analysis. During my cleanout, I discovered a box full of duplicate checks, some more than a decade old, sitting in the bin simply because we hadn't taken the time to assess their usefulness. Needing something to do and having no desire to store or move unnecessary items once again, I rip dozens of pages out of the books and listen to the roar of the shredder as I drink, and I cry.

Checks for the boys' school, rent on our New York City apartment when we lived there, the money he would give to his daughters and not tell me about. The moments of our life together were literally being chopped into a thousand pieces, month by month, year by year.

The dismantling of a marriage. The dismantling of love.

CHAPTER SEVENTEEN
CAREGIVER AGAIN

I've lost sixty degrees and added fifteen inches of snow.

Arriving at the family vacation home in northern Wisconsin, I unpack, get the cat reoriented, pull on the new sheepskin-lined boots I needed to buy for this excursion along with the puffer coat that has hidden in the back of a closet for five years, and traipse into town for groceries. This is meat and potato country, canned food country. I load my cart, picking over the plastic-wrapped vegetables, the plastic-wrapped chicken, forgoing the God-knows-how-long-it's-been-out-of-water fish. Food choice is just the first of the many adjustments I'll need to make.

Dad's duplex isn't adequate for two, so he'll be moving in with me here at the lake. Since I've traveled, I'm a COVID risk, so until I get an all clear on a test, I'm alone and have no idea what I'll be facing.

What help will my father need? What help will his pride allow? The fact that he asked, in his own vague "I don't really need it but . . ." way shows he's hesitantly facing a new reality. But I know the man, know his propensity for stubborn denial, and whatever issues he's facing will be worse than he lets on.

Back in my childhood hometown, I'm a stranger now to this rural, Northwoods life. Although I've returned many times since, it's always been as one of the many summer visitors who keep the local economy afloat with purchases of moccasins, fudge, and weekend fishing licenses. I've been a city girl for decades. In Chicago, I walk everywhere. I have three Starbucks within a ten-block radius. Here, snowmobiles and ATVs rule the road, not pedestrians. Pickup trucks are the vehicle of choice. Plaid flannel and caps are the uniforms. And the nearest Starbucks is a two-hour drive.

The Illinois plates on my car brand me as the foreigner I am.

Beautiful and serene, in theory, this place should serve to soothe my battered heart. But I've brought the demons with me, and they won't flee just because I have a lake and pine trees outside the window.

Memories of childhood pop up as I pass through the community, running the necessary errands to outfit a home rarely occupied in winter. While out, I notice that the hockey arena still stands, remodeled and expanded, conjuring fond memories of figure-skating lessons and bumblebee costumes worn during the annual ice show.

Farther down that same road, I pass the spot where my mother drowned an unwanted litter of kittens. I was five, maybe six years old, and I still know the exact spot where she pulled over on the bridge one night, the mewing kittens in a pillowcase stuffed with rocks and tied at the top that she dropped into the water below. I cried quietly in the back seat of the station wagon, my sister Sandy on the bench seat next to me, too young to know what had happened. We drove home in silence, and I ran into the dark living room, pressed my face into a corner, and sobbed. My mother ignored me. She made no effort to acknowledge what had just happened or my distress. And I never forgave her.

I hadn't pictured that night so vividly in many years. Which traumatic memories of my marriage will sit with me for decades, triggering a response both visceral and heart-wrenching? The moment in the rehab center where I learned the truth? Hearing my husband say, "It was just sex"? Walking out of therapy after calling him a self-centered prick? All of them, I suspect.

Thanksgiving is here. My first holiday alone. *Alone* alone. There is no celebration. No great bird glistening, golden and crispy on the table. No mashed potatoes oozing with butter. No hours of planning and chopping and basting. No family jokes or squabbles. No men zoned out in front of a college football game. There is not even a dried-out, overly sweet, store-bought pecan pie.

Instead of the normal festivities, I park myself on the sectional, alternating between mindless movies, a novel, and naps while my cat, Isabel, mirrors my sprawl.

Although my body succumbs to my wrenching emotional state, there is much to be grateful for. I'm healthy, my children are healthy, our finances are stable, I have dear friends. The ravages of COVID, although terrifying, have thus far spared those near and dear to me. Will that continue? I can't answer, but for now, it is worthy of the silent thank you I offer up to the universe.

My husband phones early in the day with the pretext of a Happy Thanksgiving wish and some discussion on listing our Florida condo for sale. There is work to be coordinated, timing to decide on, and pricing to agree on. The conversation didn't stay on real estate, however, and he steers the dialogue into effusive concern for my welfare. He's worried about my ability to heal as I care for my father.

"Are you staying safe? Wearing a mask? Is your dad? I'm sure no one else up there is."

Here, I'm immersed in a COVID-denying part of the country that seems to view itself as immune to its ravages. When the bar staff at the White Spruce and Lumpy's and Shotski's are all dropping like flies en masse, maybe then it will be real.

"I know you won't take me up on this, but I'll come up there if you need a break. If it gets to be too much with your dad. It's a lot for you right now. Just think about it. I'd do anything for you," he says.

My throat clenches all over again, and I can't stop the tears long enough to respond. And I believe him. At this moment, I believe if I asked, he would run to the airport and be on the next plane. The grief breaks me. It splits open the wound again, raw and oozing with regret and hurt.

How can this man who would do anything for me now be the same man who treated me like something to be scraped off the bottom of his shoe?

I have no answer to his duality, and I doubt I will ever be able to make peace with the duplicity.

Hours later, my thoughts still on his declaration, anger resurfaces. How many lies did he tell me over the years? How many lies did he tell other women? How many times did he conceal his drinking, where he was, what he was doing, who he was with? Thousands? Does he even know?

Has he been truthful to anyone, ever?

"I'll do anything for you" is about his guilt.

"You'd do anything except tell the truth and keep your dick in your pants!"

Those words come when there is no one to hear them, when they have no sting except in my heart.

194

The man who lied to me, perhaps thousands of times, is not a man who will do anything for me. He had never been a man who would do anything for me.

Or can both things be true? Can I accept that what was true then is not what is true now? Can I make peace with the ache and confusion of his duality now that booze is out of his life?

My COVID test is clear, and Dad is moving in. The man I see in front of me when I arrive at his home shocks me. It's only been a handful of months since I saw him last, and his ankles are the size of cantaloupes, his breathing labored, and he can't seem to stand without support. It's worse, far worse than he's let on.

I open the back of his pickup truck and help him load a suitcase, a trash bag he's stuffed full of clothes since he only possesses one piece of luggage, his computer bag, a cardboard box full of his favorite booze, and this odd, foot-bike-like device he has added to his daily routine after being chastised by his cardiologist for not exercising.

"What do you do with this thing?" I ask, trying to understand the function of the contraption.

"You pedal it," is his non-helpful answer. "Darlene has one."

So a stationary bike thingy that only involves the muscles of your lower legs as recommended by a friend in assisted living. I can hear the infomercial in my mind.

He follows me out to the lake, and I watch nervously as he tentatively climbs the stairs, gripping the railings with both hands. By the time he's inside, he's winded and plops down in a chair at the kitchen table while I unload and deposit his things in a bedroom on the main floor.

His early assertion, before I arrived, that he could manage multiple trips up and down stairs each day and would prefer a bedroom on the lower level—so as not to kick me out of the bedroom I normally use—was pure fantasy, as I suspected. Ego and pride haven't yet failed him, although I can't say the same about his ailing body.

I'd already ignored his "give me the small, crappier bedroom downstairs" request and had unpacked there myself. Wisely, he doesn't argue. As an added benefit, it also means I won't have to tiptoe around the house after his eight p.m. bedtime.

I was nineteen when I last lived with my father, the summer between my freshman and sophomore years of college when I returned home for a seasonal job he had arranged for me at the power company where he worked. Driving a utility truck that made me feel awkward and tiny, I had cruised the rural side roads, tagging electric poles with identifying markings, painting gas meters, scaring off snakes as they sunned on transformers, and silently battling some weekend creep who worked a separate shift and had a penchant for terribly raunchy porn mags that he would stash under the driver's seat, revealing themselves if I stopped abruptly. Whoever he was, he spent a lot of money replacing the material I discarded for him.

It seems several lifetimes ago. I was a girl—naive and young. I didn't yet know myself or what I wanted in life beyond escaping the rural existence I had been raised in. I took with me the practical, steady characteristics of this place, but experiences have shaped me, broadening my expectations. I no longer fit here.

It's hard to be here now. It's hard to see this man who was always tall and strong and confident, now hunched and swollen and resisting his need for help. He's always been the guy who fixed things, built things, took charge of anything that appeared to need him. Now, frustrated, in pain, and angry with his failing body, he is forced into unspoken acceptance. He allows me to cook, clean, run errands for him, and order bigger shoes and socks to provide relief for his immensely swollen feet. Diagnosed with lymphedema, in addition to congenital heart failure, he's wearing compression wraps on his legs that he can't put on alone and being driven weekly to a town forty-five minutes away for physical therapy. There is no cure, only attempts at improving his comfort.

His world is small, routine. Breakfast is a can of Ensure and a cookie. Lunch, spread cheese on crackers. Day after day, regardless of what I offer and the concerns I express about his diet's poor nutritional value, he wants what he wants and will entertain no other suggestions. He naps in the afternoon. Local TV news goes on at five, he switches to CNN at six, dinner is in a compromise time slot of six thirty, then he's in bed by eight. The changes in him are glaring since I last visited. He's struggling more to breathe, to stand, to walk. He's drinking sweet vermouth with lunch. Indigestion is a new constant state reminding me of my mother's condition before she learned she had pancreatic cancer.

His day drinking is new, and I don't know what to make of it. My body tenses. I flinch. It's a triggering event that reminds me of drunken ugliness. I don't know if this is something new for me to worry about or an indication of his level of pain.

And I don't know what else to do for him.

I feel helpless, yet needed. Burdened, yet burdensome. Grateful that I can be here, yet fearful of his dependence on me.

Loyalty, family, need. I'm the only family member who seemingly has nothing else pulling at her time, my dad has decided, so my siblings sit it out on the sidelines. For now. But how long can I stay when my life is already emotionally fraught? How will this play out as his condition worsens?

We watch for deer in the yard and joke about my soft streak as I toss apples to them from the deck. We laugh at the cat as she sprints through the house, enchanted by the world of squirrels and rabbits and birds outside the window. We watch the evening news together, and I listen to him complain daily that I'm making too much food for dinner. I suspect he can't remember the last time he'd eaten fruit or a vegetable that I hadn't shoved in front of him. He'd be content with canned soup and packaged lunch meat, but if he wants me to cook, I set the menu. And it isn't Oscar Mayer and Campbell's.

We're finding our way, establishing a routine. He's a reader now, plowing through my novels in a few days, the only fiction I ever recall him reading. The only books I ever recall him reading for that matter. I order everything Craig Johnson has written and move on to Steve Martini when he runs out, distributing the finished books to three different Little Free Libraries. Between reading sessions, he naps, several times a day now, and I closet myself on the lower level, trying to write, trying to manage the divorce, and wondering when I might be in a place where the pain isn't so close to the surface. Wondering what I want for my new life, whatever and whenever that might be.

In our own ways, we're both privately rebelling against the changes fighting their way into our lives. It's a stage that can only be clawed through. Him to the end of his physical life, me toward a type of rebirth.

I don't know if I believe in an afterlife or an everlasting soul. I've never faced what he's facing, never felt my heart struggling to beat. I only know a heart shattered by a husband's ultimate betrayal. Are there similarities? Perhaps.

But how do I balance my own quest for healing, which depends on a certain level of selfishness, with the demands placed on me because of my father's needs? I'm frozen in place. Literally and figuratively. Emotionally and financially.

Moments of impatience occasionally pop through, not for the man or his care, but for the holding pattern of divorce. I browse Zillow, imagining new cities, new homes. Wondering how I'll create a new life and where I want to be. Grateful that I have that choice.

Like my obsession—the obsession I still call into existence at night when I'm alone—contemplating the options is part of my lifeline. Years of indecision had pressed down on me, prevented me from looking out at the horizon, and now the road in front of me has few barriers, but also no map.

Dad and I have weathered the first month of our arrangement, settling into days filled with meal prep and leg wraps and decreasing mobility. Pain shows on his face every time he stands, every time he walks, and his exhaustion is plain to see in between. I worry about a fall and his false sense of what he can still do. I worry that he doesn't want to hear reality.

I can't help my father heal. I can only ease his discomfort, the physical and the emotional. But perhaps tending to him will help me start healing myself.

Feeling unsettled and frustrated about what might be next, I grasp at a lifeline, a lifeline I clutched at once before—Amara. We schedule a tarot reading via FaceTime. She smiles and remembers saying, "He's still lying to you," but doesn't ask how that played out. I listen to her repeat my name and shuffle the cards. This time, my hands are not tight in my lap, there is no tightness in my chest as she lays out the spread. Will this work if I'm not there, if I don't touch the cards myself? I notice she uses a different deck this time. The colors are brighter, the graphics bolder. I listen and take notes, feeling myself open up to whatever message comes through. Hoping simply for the encouraging words that reassure me I will be okay.

She doesn't use a formal spread like those filling boards on Pinterest. Cards turn, are laid down, and grouped according to some instinct within her that I can't decipher.

"Hmm, this is interesting," she says. She focuses on a small grouping of about five cards, the top card containing an image of an arched brick doorway set into a wall. A dirt path leads to the arch, lush vegetation lines the side walls, cascading over them. Mountains can be seen in the distance through the gate. And above is a bright blue sky with puffy clouds. In those clouds, a single hand cradles the Ace of Pentacles.

"I see you moving to the desert," are her next words.

I feel the smile as it washes over me. I've told no one of my Tucson fantasies. In fact, those close to me would think desert living would be out of character, yet, once again, somehow, Amara knows.

I buy a dress. A black, fitted, sexy, sophisticated, made-for-my-body, hugs-my-hips-perfectly, oh-my-God-I-look-fucking-amazing dress. In the land of moccasin shops and logoed sweatshirts, I find a dress that I simply have to have.

On a run into town for groceries, I make a quick side trip to the one store in a hundred miles that isn't Dollar General or a T-shirt shop or a chain drugstore. Why is this dress even here? It has no useful life in a community where snowmobiles and fishing boats outnumber people. Camo everything is the outfit du jour. Lululemon, Chicago's day uniform for women, would be "lulu-what? Is that a dessert?" here in the Northwoods. This is Walmart country where anything over thirty bucks is simply inconceivable. Yet this dress is here. Hanging on an upper post, tucked behind a corduroy field coat. I find the hook and lift it down off the rod mounted beyond my reach. It's my size, an unusual occurrence in itself in this part of the world.

No, I don't fit the typical midwestern, sturdily built body type. I've been blessed with being small. Independent designer boutique clothes fit me. Italian labels really fit me. Average American sizing, well, I've never been there. And genetics tells me I never will. So again, why is this dress here tucked behind the plaid and fleece?

I hold my find tight in my hand and rush to the fitting room. Perfection.

It has no purpose in my current life. It will sit unworn for months, yet I eagerly whip out the credit card without a second's hesitation before someone figures out the real value of what they're selling me, as if I've found a Jackson Pollock buried in the bins of Goodwill.

Back at the house, I contemplate what to do with my treasure. It seems too special to simply hang in the closet buried among my jeans and chunky turtleneck sweaters. I take it out of the bag, unwrap the tissue, and lay it on the bed.

I want to frame it, tuck it into a shadow box, and hang it on the wall. I want to look at it longingly, anticipating the opportunity to again become the type of woman who needs a dress like this in her life.

Staring at the simple pieces of artfully assembled cloth, I see my future. I see myself lingering over a glass of wine. I see an admiring gaze. I hear the playful conversation. I see myself past this place of pain, betrayal, and mistrust. I see myself happy.

I see hope.

Carefully, I rewrap the tissue and place the dress back in its bag in the closet, thinking I need a cedar chest to store it as if it were part of a precious dowry for my new life. Without conscious thought or explanation, I've imbued qualities into this dress far beyond the soft, sweater knit fabric and a lovely cut of the neckline.

That's a lot of responsibility riding on a yard and a half of fabric.

CHAPTER EIGHTEEN
UNSEEN

"Darlene has COVID," my father says as I walk into the kitchen.

I stop in my tracks, hoping my face doesn't convey the intensity of the fear that immediately grips me. "That means we've been exposed too," I say, looking at his fragile body, hearing his wheezy breathing, knowing that if he gets sick, this will be bad.

My father has been driving Darlene to doctor's appointments, their only in-person contact during COVID. Two days ago, I had joined them.

She was masked, as was I, but since she had tested negative on a weekly test at her assisted-living facility, Dad dismissed my suggestion that he wear a mask as well. Now, with twenty minutes of exposure in the car, Dad and I need to assume we're at risk.

"We'll need to quarantine," I say. "Do you have any appointments coming up?"

My mind scrambles, running through the mental to-do list, assuming the worst.

"Kris and Terry did okay," he says, reminding me that my sister and brother-in-law recovered from mild cases. He's conveniently ignoring his increased risk due to age and poor health.

"You should probably call your doctor and ask about testing."

He grumbles and makes faces, complaining that he can't even talk to her anyway so what's the point?

Doctors have simply become necessary but hard-to-get-ahold-of pill pushers in his mind. I can't disagree with him on that front, but toughing it out isn't an option for a frail eighty-eight-year-old man with a failing heart. Nor is COVID the place to make some half-assed ethical stand protesting your disappointment with our medical system.

Quarantine is nonnegotiable. He nods and shrugs reluctantly.

If Dad gets sick, if I get sick, I have no idea what I'll do. There is no backup plan.

I look at his thin, spider-webbed skin that maps the decades of his life. I see the stooped body that once balanced children and grandchildren on its shoulders. I see eyes that once blazed green with life, now grayed with defeat, and I can't bear the thought that he could become a statistic.

As it stands, he can no longer put on the compression wraps he wears on his feet to control his lymphedema or the socks to cover the wraps or his sneakers over the thick layers without help. Simply remaining upright in the shower is becoming problematic; he becomes exhausted from the effort of standing for just those few minutes. How would I manage a man of his size should he become ill? Or if I did?

Out of habit, I send my husband a text letting him know about the COVID exposure. He phones minutes later, wanting to know the details, trying to figure out what he can do, expressing his fear for me, offering up his Chinese medicine doctor who has some herbal protocol for immune response. His concern once again leaves me in tears, unable to speak.

I shouldn't have sent the text. The emotions bubble up in me, and I can't say anything of substance for fear of unleashing a torrent. It's too much. The divorce, Dad, COVID, my unknown future, the ugliness of my husband's past behavior. I can't seem to settle on one emotion during these "I'm worried about you" conversations. Appreciation for the concern; anger that it's now too little, too late; and the thought, *Where the hell was that concern when you were out screwing around?* all rattle around in my head. They ricochet through me as we speak. The conflicts are too great. The pain is still too raw. Emotions overwhelm me, and I cry silently on the phone. My voice cracking, I simply say thank you, afraid to release the dam of pain, anger, and disappointment.

Silence is again my preservation and the price of being collateral damage.

I hang up, call my sister, then get to work assessing our readiness for quarantine, assuming one or both of us will get sick.

Food, water, supplements, over-the-counter meds. Grocery delivery doesn't exist here, and we'll run out of fresh fruit and veggies quickly. But here in meat-and-potato land, my brothers have stocked plenty of protein in the freezer. We'll manage. The deer, well, they will simply have to be disappointed that the apple lady isn't delivering treats.

Twenty-four hours later, Dad still refuses to call his doctor. So I Google "COVID testing near me" and confirm that testing options are limited to doctor referrals. Then I check online sources for home test kits and check the latest CDC quarantine guidelines as I prepare for a ten-to-fourteen-day countdown.

"Well, I'll just go to the clinic and ask them where I can get a test," he says.

Even after our quarantine conversations, even after I've chastised him for not masking when around Darlene, he wants to go to the clinic to ask them *in person* where he can get a COVID test. In person because this is his world. He doesn't surf the internet. He doesn't make purchases online. *Google* is not a verb to him. If it's not printed in his phone book, the business doesn't exist. His computer is simply an email device, and that's a tenuous relationship at best. I swallow my "mom voice" and explain again the concept of quarantine, that we need to proceed as if we're positive and therefore shouldn't risk infecting others.

He grumbles and acquiesces. A short phone call to his clinic later, we are directed to a website where they've authorized an appointment for a COVID test. Then I excuse myself to text rant with my sister over the latest episode of "Why isn't this sinking in?"

We isolate and wait, looking for symptoms, waiting for test results, and I wonder about his future as I wonder about my own. Even if COVID doesn't hit him, his aging body and deteriorating health are taking a toll. Has he made any plans? Does he have wants? His burgeoning frailty has been cloaked by distance and children who see him over short snippets of time. He is a man who shelters his vulnerability from the world. Now it cannot be denied.

Results are in. Thankfully, we've escaped infection—Darlene was likely a false positive—but the exposure was a wake-up call. Perhaps more to me than to him. If Dad falls or gets ill, I won't be able to help him. That thought hovers perpetually in my mind as I see him struggle, feeling helpless to alleviate his suffering in any way that is permanent and lasting.

I order him a pair of bigger, wider slip-on shoes and extra-large diabetic socks. I suggest a walker or a cane, but his ego won't allow it. I order a shower chair. I investigate grab-bar installation.

Pride and denial run deep in this man. Denial of his health. Denial of his diminishing abilities. Denial that there will need to be another plan for his care, soon.

I have no experience with a body that no longer cooperates. I can't understand the loss of autonomy or dignity or the psychological impact of his physical restrictions. For now, I simply fill in the gaps between his ability and his needs and monitor for the time when his needs are beyond my skill, physically or medically.

The parent is slowly becoming the child. The child is becoming the parent.

I've always viewed my father as strong and in charge of everything. Now he is unsteady and frail, fearful of the world, and the intimacy shakes me. I don't know where this experience will lead or how long our arrangement will last, but it's clear, to me at least, he shouldn't live alone ever again. But what will that mean?

The mere mention of acquaintances in assisted living has brought expressions of outright disgust. His words to both me and my sister have been, "If I get to that point, just shoot me." Thanks, Dad. Helpful. Unfortunately, he isn't joking. What's next for him if his health deteriorates is not a decision I can make, nor is it yet time to make it. I tuck the thought back into the recesses of my mind, postponing what may become inevitable.

I am aware that in the great irony of the universe, I've moved from caring for one stubborn man who was deeply invested in denial to now caring for another. Will I be unseen here too? Will I need to divorce him too?

Christmas. It's Goddamn Christmas. It's cold and gray and sad, and I can't stop feeling sorry for myself. There is not a single gift under the pathetic plastic Charlie Brown fake tree, not a decoration in the house, not a holiday meal to prepare. There seems no point to it all this year. Dad doesn't want a celebration, and I'm too trapped inside myself to do anything. I'm alone at Christmas for the first time in decades. Just me, my dad, and the cat, and she doesn't care. It's one more day, just like the dozen that came before it. But it's not. It's a holiday. The big holiday where family is the focus and much of the country has shut down to celebrate.

Kris sends us a FaceTime call, and Dad and I sit close on the sofa, where we've spent the day in sweats and slippers, and spend a few minutes saying hello to her crew. Her husband, her kids, his kids, and the various pets have all gathered—COVID be damned—hoping the infection that struck most of them in the late fall will protect those that were not.

Warmth and contentment shine in their smiling faces, filling me with joy and jealousy. It magnifies my own loss, leaving me feeling selfish and lonely. I push down tears of regret that we can't be there with them. Regret that it's been so long since we've been able to spend time together. Regret that I can't spend time with my own kids.

Regret that I no longer have a marriage.

I have nothing to distract me today, no email needing attention, no groceries to put away, not even new snow to shovel. Worry about the future crusts over the surface of my thoughts, and for the first time since I committed to the divorce, fear and second thoughts grip me. Am I doing the right thing? Can I live with this decision? Right now, if my husband walked into the room, I fear I'd throw myself into his arms, wanting his embrace to make everything right again. And for a few minutes, it would be. For a few minutes I would forget, pushing his ugliness out of my mind so that my heart could receive the Band-Aid.

But that isn't really what I want, I know that. It's just this moment. It's just the regret over what should have been, what I wanted to be true. His embrace would merely be a temporary illusion of happiness. Buried under the raw scab that is my heart is the truth. I've been here before. Been in this place where I confuse the desire for an ice pack for something that will permanently heal the throb. Throwing myself into his arms, reneging on my decision to leave, would do nothing to heal the deep wound that has left me empty. No temporary suture will heal this.

It's the uncertainty of my life pressing down on me, making it hard to breathe. I hate this fear. Hate that it makes me feel weak. Hate feeling I have no control over my life. Hate that I must worry whether my father will be here a year from now.

My husband phones. I look at the screen, then set it aside unanswered. He leaves a voice mail wishing me Merry Christmas. I can't make myself return his call. His call is about his own sadness and guilt and loneliness, his own need to feel better. He thinks it will allow him to feel he's been a decent guy in the end, I suppose, or maybe he assumes continued contact will keep his hope alive that I might do what I've been tempted to today.

I can't talk to him today. The profuse concern that pours out of him when we speak only reminds me of what he's destroyed, magnifying my anger.

His continued "I'd do anything for you" statements magnify his willingness to discard our love.

Today I can't help him. I can't suck it up and pretend I'm fine.

I can't help him feel better at my expense. Not today.

The last day of the year is here. The end of this awful, cruel year of hell where nothing was normal, where everything thought to be true and real was turned on its head, proven to be unworthy of our confidence. I hold on to hope that 2021 will be better. That it *has to* be better. After all, what could be worse than where we have come to in this unmitigated disaster that is the US response to COVID?

What could be worse than daily body counts now routinely in the thousands? What could be worse than infection rates that have skyrocketed to unimaginable levels? What could be worse than counting another death every few minutes?

Likely, the month that will follow.

We're all tired of the restrictions, the inability to see people we love. Tired of masking and hiding and being alone. Tired of being handcuffed to our own four walls no matter how beautiful they might be. Tired of sanitizing everything we touch. Tired of worrying whether every cough, every ache, every hint of a sore throat might mean we're sick or that the person next to us in the grocery store is.

We're tired of worrying whether someone we love is going to be the next to die.

So, out of fatigue and loneliness, we've braved the airports and gathered in homes with our families or a handful of friends over the holidays. We're tired and angry and emotionally drained at a minimum. At its worst, people are sitting in hours-long lines praying that the food bank doesn't run out before they get to the front, or that they won't become homeless after being evicted in the middle of a harsh winter.

It's an easy bit of mental gymnastics to get to the place of taking the risk, assuming that you're "being careful," that a couple of hours with someone you love is worth it after all we've suffered through. It's easy to justify that this isolation and distancing is destroying our mental health, and that matters too. Perhaps if I weren't caring for an elderly man in poor health or in the middle of the pain of divorce, I, too, might be tempted to take the chance and drive down to see my sister or my kids. Even people like me with limited social needs can't be alone all the time.

Dad has been in bed for hours already as I sit with my longing, wishing for something that feels like hope. I pull out and am tempted to slip on the black dress, the one I bought not long after arriving here in Wisconsin. The dress that sits in a bag in my closet whispering that one day I will need it, that there will again be a life full of friends and restaurant meals and maybe even a date. I run my hand over the soft fabric—inhaling its promise, casting it as a beacon to the future—before folding it up and tucking it back into its place on the floor of the closet where it must stay.

Not this New Year's Eve.

I pour myself a glass of cabernet and flip through the novel I'm forcing myself to read, waiting to be sleepy. What tears or bad dreams or anger might bubble in my gut and keep me awake tonight? What loneliness might make my empty bed feel miles wide?

There is no one to kiss at midnight, no reason to watch the forced revelry in Times Square, no champagne to pour. Instead, at the stroke of midnight, I text my kids and lie in the dark listening to the neighbors set off their private fireworks. The moon, only a day past full, pokes its light through the blinds. I get out of bed and raise the shade, admiring its brilliance. The snow glistens on the ground and turns the small pines outside my window into art. Beauty, even in the middle of the ugliest of moments, the loneliest of moments, still exists. A reminder from the universe? An act of God, as some would say? I don't feel the need to label the source of this awe, but I honor it. I lie back down with a smile, allowing the moonlight to nudge away the ghosts of the past.

Like others, I find myself alternating between despair and hopefulness. Hope seems inconsistent, but perhaps it's simply a way to cope with the endlessness of the suffering and restrictions. Perhaps I hope because a sane man will soon be president and rational actions will follow. Perhaps I hope because the New Year has arrived, and New Year's Day always brings about the sense of a fresh start.

Perhaps I hope simply because I need to believe it can't get any worse.

But wishful thinking solves nothing, and the worst is not behind us despite what I want to be true. Where will the next few weeks find us, after the travel and gatherings take their toll? As redundant as it continues to sound, the reality of what's coming is unimaginable. But we've said that for months now.

I struggle to contain my anger as I see the mask-less revelry, the overwhelmed hospital staff, the lines at food banks, the endless suffering all compounded unnecessarily by selfishness.

Yet somehow, life must go on. We can't stay frozen in place for years.

I watch my father's face as he struggles to stand without support; the simple act drains him so thoroughly that he seems on the verge of passing out. Will he get COVID? Will his heart fail first? There is no sign that vaccinations are imminent in this part of the country, and I worry endlessly about his fate.

Ego and pride rage in his mind, battling a body that knows neither, refusing to acknowledge restriction or loss while he bristles at the contradiction of needing my help.

He makes sly comments about the imagined interruption to my life caregiving has brought, then minutes later, asks me to write a check for him as his hand is now unsteady.

I bind his feet in compression wraps each morning, the skin swollen and blotched and nearly unrecognizable. It's beyond his mobility and energy level to reach down and wriggle socks over the lumpy bandaged flesh. He seems to sleep more each day.

One morning this week, I got up a bit late after a night with little sleep and found him back asleep on the sofa at eight thirty, having been out of bed himself for not much more than an hour. I made my tea, showered, and dressed, then had breakfast before returning to my lower-level lair to do some work. He slept through it all while my eyes instinctively went to his chest to confirm he was still breathing. And yesterday, I found him at the kitchen table, head down, asleep, his lunch in front of him unfinished.

Is that how he'll die? Simply falling asleep in his chair, never to awake? I think we both hope so. This past year, of all years, so many died utterly alone or surrounded by hospital staff instead of loved ones, with masked strangers doing their best with FaceTime goodbyes and a gloved hand held tight.

His fear of needing assisted living is palpable, but what options will he tolerate as the decline continues? Despite my attempts to broach the subject, he refuses to discuss it, refusing to accept what seems next in the progression.

Perhaps that's a gift. Perhaps not conceding to what others view as inevitable decline will keep him strong.

Perhaps the blinders of self-delusion or optimism or flat-out wishful thinking are keeping both of us going. Perhaps the blinders I wore to preserve my love are no different from his blinders now.

CHAPTER NINETEEN
REBELLION

Today is my anniversary. Twenty-five years. Weeks ago, nervously anticipating the event, I imagined that I would spend the day anxious, sad, and teary—agonizing over the good, the bad, the tender parts of our history. I thought I would have been tempted to jot off an angry text reminding the son of a bitch that he had thrown away the best thing in his life, that I would jam a sharp stick into his wound trying to make him hurt as much as I do. I imagined that I would do anything I could to make my pain loud, ugly, and impossible for him to ignore.

Then I imagined myself wrapped in his arms, my head tucked under his chin, feeling his chest as it rose with each breath and feeling the warmth of contentment.

Instead, the significance of the day passed almost without notice.

Now I sit late at night, alone again in my basement space as I am every night, wondering what I should make of the slight. I'm out of my element, my world is foreign and small and contained. Place and time are warped. COVID lockdown and isolation in northern Wisconsin has caused one day to blend into the next, only punctuated by trips to the grocery store or the dump. I stare at the walls, feeling untethered and disconnected from everything I thought to be true. Why should the significance of this day be different?

Tears come as the aloneness crushes me. But not anger. Not the full-on rage that occasionally boils up when *How could he?* slams into my brain. When I'm forced to face the worst questions: Did he ever love me? Was he ever capable? Does he know what love is, really?

The questions skid and slide in my mind the way they have on and off for years now. The duality an infinity scarf of the unanswerable. Yet today, on this day of all days, I can't set them aside, and I also can't bear to ponder their futility. Instead, when the pain breaks through the surface I push down the split-personality of his love with the thought, *He simply didn't love himself.* Whatever it was that he felt, whatever it is that he tells himself now, his love was not my love. It was some lesser version.

I was wrong. The rage comes at 4:18 a.m. It tears into my dreams, pushing out my obsession, intruding where I don't want it. I try to drag it back down into the recesses of my mind, into its pit, to suppress it because I don't want to feel its rawness anymore. I try to move back into the sweet release of tenderness from another man who would never lie, of an imagined life without the haunting history of pain. But the rage will not shake. I lie in the dark, my bedding a tangled mess, the moon casting an eerie shadow through the blinds, awash in memories of the moment I knew the truth. Memories of the fury that ate away at my insides. Memories of so many moments when I stared at the floor holding my rage and my hurt close, because I couldn't face my pain mirrored in the eyes of others.

I've never been able to forgive myself for that weakness, for my silence. A weakness that I still can't explain in any way that soothes my anger and disappointment in myself.

Now, in the middle of the night on my twenty-fifth anniversary, I pull my laptop off the desk onto the bed and let my fingers fly across the keyboard, needing to say it all. Needing to document my anguish, my memories, and my disgust with myself. Hoping, I suppose, that by recording it, it will release. But as I write, I'm left wondering which pain will stay with me longer, the pain inflicted on me or the pain of my inaction?

Yet I engaged in the secrets by not calling them out. By not making myself loud with hurt. And if I am truthful, with myself anyway, my silence contributed to the lie.

Silence was my protection.

They say that time heals all wounds. Does it heal or simply blunt the pain, the ache instead becoming a constant roar that we no longer distinguish from the other roars assaulting our bodies and minds?

I can't answer. Not tonight. Not on this day.

For five years, I've fought an internal battle between love and hate. Hate for how easily his deficiencies allowed him to discard me, allowed him to compartmentalize his behavior into something without consequences. His thoughts, apparently, were only on his immediate want. And whether he saw it that way in the confused moments when I forced him to hear my pain, it was a discarding.

I assume the alcoholic mind can't fully step outside itself to find objectivity even after the booze is gone. It's been rewired, morphing into something full of boxes that don't touch, refusing to understand the relationship between cause and effect, behavior and consequence. It's all want and need and impulse, everyone else be damned.

217

Even in this awful moment as I'm again torn open, I still know it was never about me. More accurately: part of me knows that. The part that is the good girl, the smart, understanding wife, the has-her-shit-together woman; she knows. The part of me with the broken, bleeding, shredded, will-I-ever-be-whole-again heart; she just thinks he was a self-centered prick.

The duality in me is also impossible to live with, and once again I sit alone in a dark room, in a bed that isn't mine, in a home I don't want to be in, regurgitating it all over and over in my mind. When will it end? When will my mind accept that I cannot understand?

It's not the disease nor the betrayals nor the fear of what I still do not know that haunts me now. What consumes me is, despite how much I loved him and how much he believed he loved me, how I was affected by the consequences of his actions did not matter to him.

That is not love. Certainly not the kind of love I want and deserve.

Therein lies the conflict on this, my twenty-fifth anniversary. I'm left uncertain if I was ever loved, or if the love I thought I was receiving was nothing more than my desire for it. Did I fabricate his love in the same way I've fabricated my obsession?

What I do believe is that love is precious. It doesn't find us easily or often. But when it does enter our lives, it should be exchanged freely, nurtured, and fought for. Love is stubborn. It refuses to fade quickly. It takes a toehold and hangs on for dear life, as it should. But love can also destroy. It can exist even when it siphons the life out of us leaving an empty shell, a void filled with false promises, and one who has been diminished at another's expense.

Love is not something to be suffered through. It is something to be mutually cherished. If that love is harmful and one-sided, it is brave and necessary to leave it behind for the dream and promise of another chance, for the dream of something equal and honest.

Real love, special love, is always worth waiting for. You just have to be ready to recognize it.

It isn't the question I expected to be contemplating on the eve of my twenty-fifth anniversary, but will that love ever find me? Or will I again allow want to blind me?

———————

Dad has that old man smell now. A faintly sour, end-of-life odor immediately recognizable to anyone who has spent time in an assisted-living facility where it mingles with the acrid scent of disinfectant. His fragile skin is blotched and spotted and easily bruised. His legs and feet swell, expanding until constrained by the compression wraps he wears, leaving them lumpy, misshapen, and lacking sensation.

I no longer need to ask if he wants a ride to his doctor's appointments or hear him insist that he doesn't need the help. The task of chauffeur is now assumed to be mine. There has been no discussion about the shift; we've simply accepted it as fact.

He's begun sharing the details of his death plan—instructions for what to do in the event "something happens to me." He tells me, "Tom has access to my bank account. My plot is next to Bonnie and Sandy. Here are the passwords to my important online accounts." He shares these things sporadically, working bits of information into everyday conversation as easily as we discuss the day's weather or the latest deer sighting. I take it in without emotion, accepting his need to plan, to make what is inevitable easier for his children to manage. But inside I wonder, *Does he know something? Does he feel it coming? Is he tracking the slow failure of his heart? Will he die the way he wants to—quickly, easily, never reaching the place of drool and feeding tubes and someone else wiping his backside? Or will he fade slowly and helplessly over what will seem like a cruel eternity?*

It is unknowable but impossible not to contemplate. I feel both the gift and burden of being with him. At moments I'm grateful; at moments, anxious to leave; at moments, guilty.

But I am constrained, attached to a leash outside of my control. I'm held in place not only by my father's needs but by a divorce not yet resolved, by property not yet sold, by COVID that cautions against travel when I crave exploration of new places to live, a way to imagine whatever will be next for my life.

My mind and spirit rebel, needing an emotional release. A trip to Tucson has been on the calendar for quite some time. A trip I planned with my dear friend Ann for the Gem Show, long before I knew with certainty that I would divorce, long before the unexpected detour for my father's care, long before the events now rocking the news cycle. The show has been postponed, and Ann has changed her mind about the trip, nervous about going at all—nervous about COVID.

I, on the other hand, am not changing a damn thing. It's just two weeks out, and the hotel's been long booked, the flight, the rental car, my sister coming in to care for Dad—everything is arranged.

The need to escape floods my thoughts. Yet it feels both selfish and as essential for my mental health as breathing is to my body. But COVID. Will I selfishly bring COVID back with me?

I can't not go. The urgency of my need for this trip invades my cells. The thought of canceling is even more painful than being locked here in Wisconsin. Tucson has held my thoughts, intriguing me, as I try to envision a life for myself beyond this limbo, using my imagination as a bridge to a place where the pain is gone. I need something, a glimmer of something, to keep me from sinking back into nothingness.

And this trip is a chance to test whether the thoughts have weight.

I stalk real estate listings online trying to imagine myself in this new place. Crunching numbers in my head, I try to mentally negotiate what the compromises in size or quality or neighborhood might be now that I'll be a family of one. I dream and pull tear sheets for future design work. Can I find an old adobe to rehab? Do I remodel something worn and tired? Do I build new?

I don't even know if Tucson is the place I want to settle, but for now it serves as a placeholder, something for me to picture.

They seem frivolous things: the layout of a kitchen or the strain of living with dated bathrooms desperate for a remake. But to me they are not minor, they are symbols, stand-ins for stability and safety. These details are the things that buttress the gap between my old life and my new—the transition point to making myself comfortable after I shed this skin. Home is my grounding point, my foundation. And right now, these tenuous plans fuel me. They are the light of daydreams and promises of a life without regret. They give me something to hold on to as I work through the restraints and must-dos and tangle of lists while I wait for my bindings to loosen.

It is the first full moon of 2021. The Day of Miracles according to astrologers. And my first full day in Tucson. I arrived late yesterday afternoon at a small, intimate downtown inn that is even more charming than I imagined after studying the photos online. Tall beamed ceilings, terracotta floors, comfortable, welcoming furniture, a stunning courtyard, history. It's perfect. The owner greets me, and it's as if I've walked into her home, a home I want to stay in and never leave.

With COVID still raging and the Gem Show canceled, I'm the only guest—an odd but delightful situation. Already I'm at ease, instantly imagining myself living in a place like this, feeling myself sink into a new life.

In the morning, breakfast is served in the great room as I sit at a carved oak table sipping my Earl Grey tea. Yogurt with fruit and pistachios, scones lightly flavored with almonds, and eggs delicately scrambled follow. The setting is so intimate I feel embarrassed to be waited on. In minutes, the manager—Dora—and I learn we have a shared background in fashion, and we drink tea and talk for an hour and a half. I feel like I've made a new friend. Tucson is welcoming me, showing me her capacity for love.

It's been almost a year since I've traveled, dined in a restaurant, had social contact with anyone but my husband and father. A year of fear and worry. A year of emotional pain and indecision. A year of uncertainty. I slip in and out of all those emotions as I envelop myself in this beautiful place while hope also flirts around the edges.

I spend the afternoon walking for miles, exploring the historic neighborhood, journeying past homes I'd bookmarked on Zillow for consideration. I admire the strong, simple architectural shapes of the adobe walls, the colorful washed plaster, and creative ironwork gates. I dine on tacos in an outdoor courtyard restaurant, revisiting a haunt from my last trip here as if I'm a local. It's foreign and exciting and exhilarating to imagine my online dreaming as a new reality.

As I admire the adobe homes, memories of my marriage also flood in. I'm drawn back to a Georgia O'Keeffe exhibition we attended at the Brooklyn Museum, its wistful images of Ghost Ranch and another desert life mirroring this landscape. My thoughts turn to an equally charming inn we stayed at in Lenox, Massachusetts, when we toured MASS MoCA and the Frelinghuysen Morris House. Then I remember the way his eyes light up when he smiles. The solidness of his chest when I laid my head on his shoulder to fall asleep.

Thoughts and emotions somersault with no pattern or consistency, dragging me between my past and my imagined future. It's the middle I'm missing, the now. Because now is limbo. Now is waiting. Now is nothingness. I don't exist here.

I try to shed the skin of my past, but the molting is incomplete. Whatever lies underneath the mangy, ragged shell is unknowable. I can't yet see its form. I don't know what part of the old DNA will travel with me and what part will sprout new, born from the pain.

Perhaps that's the reason having a sense of place has become so important. It's concrete, knowable; it has a form that I can see and turn over in my mind, imagining how I might fit into it. Even though the location of my future home is not certain, imagining it gives me a framework in which to feel safe.

Later, back at the inn, wine and spiced nuts are waiting. I lounge in the lush courtyard on a cushioned chaise, feet up, a glass in my hand, feeling content and excited. A fountain gurgles gently; a soft breeze brushes my face as hummingbirds flit in and out of the lavender lining the brick patio. I imagine this as my life while I flip through tourist magazines and scroll real estate listings. Nearly every home on my saved list has suddenly gone under contract in the two days since I last looked. The spring boom has begun in earnest fueled by the COVID surge and as a twinge of panic hits. I'm weeks, perhaps months, out from being able to commit to either the city or property, and the idea of homes going under contract almost instantaneously doesn't fit with my reality.

Still, I spend my time exploring. Systematically working from the city center out, neighborhood by neighborhood, I drive, look, and drive some more. I roam the streets, ogling buildings, until security patrols and homeowners wonder whether I'm a real estate agent or scoping out the place for theft. Barrio Viejo, Armory Park, Sam Hughes, El Encanto, Colonia Solana—neighborhoods full of charm and history. I wander and wonder and imagine, trying to picture myself in this place.

I spend days up in the foothills where neighborhoods are newer, gated, and often centered around a golf course. I don't golf. I haven't lived in a gated community. I live in a large city high-rise. Everything about home is foreign here. The old adobes, the grand Spanish-influenced architecture, the suburban contemporaries infused with southwestern touches and magnificent mountain views.

Cautiously, I seek out grocery stores, art supply stores, furniture stores, garden centers, and bookstores, trying to place my daily life into the framework of this city, trying it on for size. A shop owner strikes up a conversation, offers guidance, and passes on a realtor's name. A gallery owner suggests other galleries to visit. I eat tacos and guacamole daily and order grilled artichokes every time I find them listed on a menu. I have wine with lunch while scrolling Zillow on my iPad as I sit at outdoor cafés, feeling decadent and alive.

I'm alone but not lonely, buoyed by the friendliness of everyone I've encountered. After months of caring for my father, months of COVID isolation, months of agonized decision-making over whether to divorce, I'm out in the world as an almost-single woman, contemplating a new life in a new place.

I expected to feel apprehension about the idea of life in a new town where I have little history and few connections, but there is none. Perhaps it's simply the joy of being out in the world again or the thought that someday my life will be defined as more than a woman divorcing, a caregiver to my elderly father, a writer who is uninspired to write at the moment. I can't know what will hit me along the way, but for now, I feel content. There is a time in front of me where I will feel at peace again, where I will find my center again, where I will emerge from the pain and remember the woman I once was. Where I will become the new version of that woman, the version of myself that is no longer angry or hurt. The woman who can again live in joy. She's out there. I can feel her ghost now. I see glimpses of her at moments, like a spirit that wants to latch onto life, hoping to become flesh and blood.

Toward the end of my trip, I return to the inn one evening, and Dora and I sit in the courtyard with a glass of wine enjoying another day of perfect weather. As women who quickly connected, our conversations have skipped the mundane and gone straight to the heartfelt.

She is studying metaphysics and tries to share with me the abstract concepts of time and space and causality in that world. Some aspects strike a logical chord with me, other points require an abandonment of what feels concrete, and I struggle to understand the elusiveness of the concepts. Or perhaps I struggle to discard the dogma of what I've assumed to be true.

She looks at me and says, "In my belief system, everything that happens in life is something that we brought to ourselves."

I feel myself recoil. I feel myself cringe with horror. I feel anger bubble inside my chest that I try to hide. Not anger at Dora but at the suggestion that somehow I wanted this to happen or did something to cause this pain. And I don't know how to respond.

I take a sip of my wine, processing, stalling, struggling with her words. I simply say, "I have a hard time accepting that version of reality."

She nods, then tries to explain in new words that don't make the concept any clearer. But she doesn't know what she's asking me to assume responsibility for either.

I sit with her words, rejecting them late into the night, disgusted with the suggestion that I did something that contributed to my husband's behavior.

Did I bring my husband's alcoholism or his infidelity into my life? That's beyond my ability to accept, but perhaps I can accept that dealing with his weaknesses is making me a better version of myself. Perhaps I can accept that I needed to strengthen my backbone. Perhaps the truth is not that I caused this but that there has been something in me that needed to be rebuilt.

CHAPTER TWENTY
THE HOUSE

I've fallen in love. In love with a house.

A beautiful, beat-up, majestic adobe with an overgrown yard, a screen door hanging by one hinge, paint dirty and worn, and windows covered from the inside. She's gorgeous underneath the neglect and the filth. Vacant, likely for years. Yet the noble structure is sturdy, holding up to the abuse, daring the world to break her spine. I can feel the love buried in her plaster walls crying to be reawakened, just like my own.

Like me, she is alone and feeling the loss of love. Has she been betrayed as well? Abandoned in the slow drip of another's self-destruction? Has she, too, become collateral damage at the hands of the man she devoted herself to?

She once felt love's gentle caress, as did I. I can sense it. She felt her heart swell with the contentment only adoration can bring. I can feel her heart still beating, faint but steady, her history paralleling my own.

Like most women, she waits, expecting someone to appreciate her. Waiting for the right person to appreciate her.

But he didn't, couldn't.

Was she, too, undone by the one she loved, undone by the man who whispered his devotion, then shredded her heart as his demons rendered him incapable of offering more than hollow words?

Was her destruction swift, a quick sword to the heart? Or was it like mine? A slow bleed, love leaching out drip by almost imperceptible drip until, one day, she was an empty shell of what she had once been.

Staring at her graceful frame, I see no cracks in the foundation, no chipped stucco, no rotting wood. But she hasn't felt a gentle touch or the caress of admiring eyes in far too long. For perhaps a decade or more, she hasn't heard laughter or ecstasy or tears within her walls. She hasn't watched a family prepare a meal together or seen a vase of flowers placed on the table just because it was Tuesday. She waits patiently to be recognized for her quiet beauty and resilience.

Her soft moan of neglect whispers to me. I return, visiting this spot four times during the week, parking out in front on the quiet Tucson street lined with palm trees, admiring the subtle elegance, imagining what she was in her past and what she could be again if she were loved. Googling the address gives me the basics on the square footage, taxes, the year she was built, and the number of bedrooms. I find complaints filed with the city going back years: neighbors dissatisfied with the weed-infested yard and the disarray scarring their small historic community. Digging further still, I find a name. An owner. As well as an obituary. Are they the same?

I long to go inside, imagining weathered beams and terracotta floors crying out to have their luster restored. I imagine hand-painted tiles, arched doorways, and carved doors. Or a roof that has fallen through, spreading mold and rot, turning historic charm into something unsalvageable. Enthralled, I push aside the foliage and walk the grounds, snaking through to the garden in the back, seeking a window to peer through, but they're covered; the wall to the terrace, too high; the gate to the driveway, too opaque.

But I can imagine myself inside, my abstract paintings adorning the walls, soft upholstered sofas carefully arranged in front of the stone fireplace waiting for a cool evening, a library of books lining one wall, silky wool carpets on the floor. I see my children visiting for a Thanksgiving celebration, a day rich with food, laughter, and memories. I see new friends gathered on the patio for wine and conversation on a cool evening as music plays softly in the background—a book club, perhaps.

I see a life forged out of the rubble.

This is the house. She's waiting. She's waiting for me. And I am waiting for her.

We can save each other. We can find love again; we can lean on each other for support.

We share the echo of loss, this house and I. Love that once filled us has turned rancid; decay threatens to eat away at whatever remains. As I watch her, I can hear her secrets. She can hear mine. She whispers, her voice low, unaccustomed to the attention, having been discarded so long ago. Yet she longs to live again. Longs to envelop someone in a loving embrace. Longs to share the love she is capable of. I can feel it pulsing in her the way it pulses in me. It's not too late.

I've begun to prune my damaged heart, surgically cutting away the diseased flesh, hoping the invasion of lies and betrayals during my marriage that starved my cells of fuel can be stopped before it drains me completely.

Can the beating of love return and course through my veins, rebuilding me once again? I think so. I'm here holding flickers of a future, seeing glimpses of a new life. A new home. A new city. Surely, I haven't been so destroyed that regeneration is no longer possible.

I look at this beautiful wreck of a home and see the ghost of my past. I see the woman I was before the lies and betrayals in my marriage diminished me. I see the outline of the woman I am meant to become. She is there. Waiting. Quietly. Patiently.

I don't know if this house can be mine. I don't know if we will have the chance to save each other, but she has presented me with a gift. The gift of longing.

Grudgingly, I must say farewell. It's my last night in Tucson before I must return to the frigid Wisconsin winter where I will again care for my elderly father. I take my gift with me, deciding it deserves a treat. A farewell, till-I-see-you-again dinner. I pull out the dress. The black made-for-me dress I stumbled on not long after arriving in Wisconsin. The evening is a bit too warm for the soft, knit fabric, and it's a bit too far to walk in heels, but I wear it anyway, needing the luxury. I need a night of wearing lipstick—even if it's under a mask—a night that I can hold onto in my memory as I work through the next few difficult months, a night where I feel the possibility of a new life. A night where I sit and imagine a life where my pain is long in the distance.

I'm seated at a café table in the walled garden of a historic restaurant, a delicate breeze teasing my hair. Decorative lights shimmer overhead, casting small shadows that dance across the brick patio. Soft jazz drifts in the background. A glass of a lovely cabernet is perched in front of me.

Closing my eyes, I inhale the heady blackberry notes of the wine, remembering evenings before I knew the truth of my marriage when a place like this would have been part of our routine. Remembering nights of laughter and conversation and tenderness.

This restaurant is a place for knowing smiles, fingers that trail slowly over an outstretched hand, intense gazes that hint at an evening of hot breath and soft moans. It's a place for lovers. And I'm the lone single woman, feeling immensely out of place and completely at home. It's a night and place of normalcy and promise. I can sit in the lush evening air, set my mask aside, and know this will again be part of my world. Something so simple, yet so special, viewed now through newly appreciative eyes.

I feel appreciation for the struggle of the business owners hanging on by a financial thread through the shutdowns, appreciation for the staff putting themselves at risk through exposure to people like me, appreciation for the small moment of something resembling human contact. I sink into it, reveling in and savoring each bite of roasted artichoke bathed in tahini, of each morsel of chicken and white beans. Nothing has tasted this good in recent memory, made even more delicious by the brief respite from harsh winters and divorce lawyers and obligations, and a demanding elderly man with a failing body.

There can be life again for me if I allow it to find me. If I push aside the pain. I saw that today as I looked at the grand adobe. I felt her love, and I felt my love in return. I heard her whispers of want and need, her desire to not lie fallow and neglected any longer.

And I felt love for myself. However it happens, whenever it happens, I will be healed. I will again be a woman filled with joy and love, no longer shackled by the harm of another.

Loneliness flirts at the edges of my mind as the couples on the terrace remind me of better days and moments when I, too, was blind to the world outside someone else's eyes. The regret is there as is the knowledge that it didn't have to be this way. I didn't deserve what I was dealt. I loved with all my heart. I swallow hard, inhale deep, and push those thoughts back down into whatever dark recesses might hold them strong.

Not tonight. Not this trip. I will not wallow in pain or anger or resentment. Tonight is about my future. Even if I'm only able to glimpse it for a few luscious moments.

CHAPTER TWENTY-ONE
LIES WE TELL OURSELVES

"Not too much!" my father says as I scoop chili I've fussed over for hours into bowls for our dinner. He's said those words more times than I can count during the long months I've been caring for him. He prefers to subsist on crackers and orange-colored spread pretending to be cheese and canned liquid meal substitutes, all squeezed between regular doses of cookies and toffee and ice cream and booze. Dinner is the one meal a day he allows me to cook.

Today it grates on me. Not the portion size or the unappreciated effort I've put into the meal or even the knowledge that I'm trying to cater to his former tastes in food instead of my own; it's the constant reminders. As if, somehow, I've forgotten after being told the ninety-nine previous times that he has little appetite. Or maybe it's his assumption that I'll be offended if he leaves three mouthfuls untouched.

Then dish up your own damn chili! forms in my mind. Of course I don't say it, and I'm annoyed with myself for even thinking it, then annoyed with myself for being annoyed, and halfway to an apology that I hadn't read his mind precisely enough.

No, Dad, I just want you to eat something I don't have to look up in a chemistry dictionary. Another thing left unsaid. Another moment where I bite my tongue.

He's obsessed with his loss of appetite, reminding me again and again that he doesn't know why he's not hungry. He's unwilling to discuss the issue with his doctor, expecting another vague answer, another pill, another dismissive, "You're old, what do you expect?" response from someone half his age.

While the outcome of a conversation with a physician may predictably lead to another pill added to his arsenal, Dad is still of the "doctor is God don't question the man" era. He is given things, prescribed things, told to do things, to not do things by doctor after doctor in the chaotic way that only our medical system can. It's all accepted without question or a moment's thought. The doc says it, and he shrugs and says okay, never understanding what or why, trotting out of the office, prescription in hand ready to add another med to the dozen he already takes. It wouldn't occur to him to question a doctor, even if the purpose was simply to understand.

I nod and smile.

I've been back in Wisconsin living with my father for all of five days, and impatience and irritation cover me like a cloak when what I want is wings. I'm short-tempered and snippy or silent, feeling chained to a place I don't want to be, caring for another helpless man, and forced again to suppress my own needs.

Ten additional inches of snow fell, shrouding the trees and burying roads, while I basked in Arizona sunshine. Any temperature above zero in the Northwoods, a frigid wall of white, would be cause for short-sleeved celebration by the locals. Not even my deer have come out to say hello, beg for apples, and gift me with a few minutes of their grace.

My world has again become small.

Each trip into town reminds me why I left this life behind as a girl. How I have changed. How I no longer fit here.

But where do I fit now?

For one glorious ten-day span, I had tasted a future, only to have that door closed on me. I've been pulled back into a world of caring for a man while my needs are pushed back into the shadows. I stomp and pout, biting back rude comments. I'm angry with myself for my impatience, angry with my father for his neediness, angry with my soon-to-be ex-husband for his selfishness, angry with divorce attorneys for not working fast enough, angry that real estate to be sold hasn't gone under contract, angry that I feel trapped without a creative outlet or a plan or a foreseeable end.

Each annoyed minute stokes the guilt and frustration I feel. It's not Dad's fault he's elderly and restricted. I agreed to do this. I wasn't forced. I could leave, I suppose, but that guilt would burn deeper still. Most days, I recognize the time as the gift to both of us that it is, but since returning from Tucson, my emotions and my wants blaze anew near the surface, and I can't seem to tamp them down.

Or maybe I'm afraid to. Surrendering to the reality of now feels like giving up or giving in to something not of my choosing.

A man, a different man, is controlling how and where and what I do.

I should take solace in my internal rebellion, I suppose. It feels important, as if I'm taking a step toward healing. It's a hint of independence. A recognition that I desire the choice rather than accepting what has been dealt me. But my future is only a shimmer of something now, too ephemeral to have form.

Dad seems to sense my frustration, giving me a wide berth at moments, biting back at others, although he'd never ask me directly how I feel. He doesn't do things like that, would never inquire about something as nebulous as my emotional state. Midwestern men who came of age in the '40s and '50s simply don't exist on that plane.

Late to preparing dinner one night this week, I explained I'd been on the phone with a girlfriend for over an hour, and he scrunched his face in confusion, unable to comprehend how two people could possibly have so much to talk about.

He tries to show me that he can manage alone, prepping me—I'm certain he believes—to feel comfortable moving on, leaving him to tend to his own needs alone in his own home. Since he struggles to put on his leg wraps without me, he's testing the waters by not wearing them at all—asking me to find him larger, less-compressing compression socks as a substitute. He'll treat his lymphedema with a wish and a prayer. I order the damn socks, knowing that lifting his foot and wrangling the bondage device on his own won't go well. But this is a conclusion he'll need to draw himself.

The daughter is not yet the mother.

Impatient that I haven't come upstairs prepared to go to the landfill ten minutes before we had agreed we were leaving, he is standing in the doorway with a broom pushing snow off the deck. I chase him away and don my outdoor gear. While I clear a safe path and brush snow off his truck for the drive, he carries two small bags of trash down icy stairs. And he does these things with an open jacket, no boots, no hat, and no gloves in fifteen degrees below zero temperatures.

Yeah, Dad, your "I'm fine, really" campaign is very convincing.

The battle between independence and physical discomfort rages illogically inside him. I can't feel what he feels, can't know his truth.

But the world of his past when he lived alone and unattended is likely gone. How do I help him face that?

Already I sense the struggle looming on the horizon. This man will not move gracefully into a place where ego and vulnerability take a backseat to safety and the concerns of his children.

Memories of tough, pleading conversations in my marriage flood back; the parallels are not of addiction but male pride and silence and definitions of weakness. The reminders lie heavy, triggering guilt and worry and hurt. They do nothing to ease my ache.

Dad and I have reached the strained marriage stage of our relationship. Outbursts? Check. Stony silence? Also check. And separate rooms as often as possible. It's the push and pull of a man rebelling against his burgeoning frailty and of a daughter terrified of what lies ahead or what she might have to deal with if a fall becomes a broken hip, a call to 911, then assisted living.

Another Saturday, another trash day. It's 9:50 a.m., and I'd gathered, bagged, and deposited trash in the garage an hour earlier, then returned to my computer to answer a few emails. Once again, ten minutes before the hour, I hear noises. This time, the man—the eighty-eight-year-old elderly man with heart failure and legs so weak he can't stand up long enough to shower—is outside, trying to load the trash into the bed of his pickup truck because I haven't arrived to do so at the precise moment he believed it had to be done. I storm outside into the ten-degree temperatures, coatless, gloveless, and wearing slippers to chastise the fool for his lack of safety concerns. Ice coats the blacktop, but he doesn't see it.

I bark at him to get in the truck while I do the heavy lifting. "Didn't we have this conversation last Saturday? Let me do this!" I yell.

Grumbling, freezing, furious, I raise my voice at the man for the first time ever. I slam the pickup gate closed, go back inside, throw on boots and a parka, and fume all the way to the landfill while he tries to make small talk and jokes.

The landfill visit is no better. I pull heavy bags out of his hands and instruct him to talk to the dump attendant who spends his time chain-smoking, chatting up old people, and handing out dog treats to the many pups who tag along.

Rinse and repeat. Upon our return, my words from two hours earlier forgotten, he tries to carry groceries up the icy walk and icy stairs. Again, I grab the bags from his hands and order him to get in the house like he's a four-year-old who wants to play in the yard without pants.

Days earlier, he had fallen on this same walkway. Knocked into the snowbank by a falling chunk of compacted snow from the roof, he couldn't get himself up, nor could I lift him. Rummaging in the garage for something to give him leverage while he lay gloveless in the frigid snow pile with a lump on his head, I found an old folding chair. I parked it in the bank for stability and got him to his feet.

He has seemingly forgotten all of this as he attempts a replay.

Dad inside, the truck unloaded, I take the shovel to knock down another snow brick on the roof before he gets hit in the head again, and suddenly I'm being chastised for exhibiting risky behavior while he feels the urge to supervise. I then yell, "What exactly are *you* going to do if I fall?"

It was not our finest hour.

Rebellion and fear—that's our tug of war. I think I'm trying to see the situation through his eyes. Trying not to use my mom voice. Trying not to tell him what he can and can't do unless safety is an obvious issue. Can he see through my eyes? Can he understand my worry?

After dinner, I serve his nightly bowl of ice cream—vanilla, always vanilla—and broach the subject that has been tumbling through my head.

"What are your thoughts about help after I leave?" I ask after he spoons the last bite and hands me the empty bowl because it's easier than standing, walking, rinsing, and opening the dishwasher four feet away.

"I'll be fine," he says. "I can get by."

I look at him, watching for hesitation, for some hint in his eyes that he senses his own vulnerability. It's a skill well practiced on another man at another time on another issue, but tonight I'm not hunting for signs of inebriation.

"You fell, Dad. You couldn't get up. I couldn't get you up. What would you have done if you were alone?"

He explains in painstaking detail how he would have crawled to the stairs and phoned his friend George. His answer is firm and definitive as if he's practiced this. As if he expected me to ask. And again, I'm reminded of carefully rehearsed stories spoken when the truth was inconvenient. Dad is lying to himself. He believes he can manage, convincing himself of this theory as he voices it. The lies my husband told himself were deeper and darker, but also dangerous. Lies that he wasn't an alcoholic. Lies that his affairs meant nothing. Lies that there would be no consequences. Lies that I wouldn't leave him.

Lies that he wasn't deserving of love.

Exasperated, I ask my father, "Then why did you ask me to come? Why am I here?"

"Now wait a minute. I didn't ask," he says.

What? You didn't ask?

In this moment, I know this is all going to go badly. I probe, ask what-if scenarios, and the answers are all some version of "I'm fine for now. I'll wait until something happens to make a plan." Apparently, the use of a full-time housekeeper, chef, cleaning lady, chauffeur, and occasional medic in the form of his daughter over the last several months is just a nice perk and doesn't reflect on his need. Ah, denial, my dear friend. Another trait I've encountered before.

For the first time, I fully understand my mother's bristling at his bossy, father-knows-best ways. And I'm right there with her. I can see the look of disdain she would shoot at him when he'd been on a do-it-my-way rant; I can hear a snarky remark that left him seething. I hope my expression isn't as telling.

But I recognize the sentiment.

And my increasing intolerance for male ego and arrogance.

It's as if a switch has been flipped, and men treating women with disrespect to soothe their own overly inflated sense of self releases a flood of intolerance in me. A dumb, sexist joke by my unenlightened father, a politician—or five—who've been newly accused of sexual harassment, snips of remembered conversation, or behaviors from my own marriage have become triggering bombs. Not that I discounted sexism in the past, but the behavior was met more with a disgusted eye roll than a flame thrower. Now it's "shut that crap down before I take you out."

Dad and I sit in the living room one evening just like all others, he with his old-fashioned, me with my wine, watching the evening news as sexual harassment accusations are made against Governor Cuomo. My father yells at the TV, "They just want money!"

My first reaction was silent rage. My second, to walk out of the room. I act on instinct. Another silence.

But I come back, spitting mad, trying to explain to this elderly man that his daughters had also been treated this way. We had been touched and propositioned and pressured for sex by men we didn't want. That in calling these accusers liars, he was calling his daughters liars as well.

His blank look tells me everything. I see confusion at my outrage, confusion that I would take this personally, confusion that his views of women are being challenged. He's old, set in his ways, distrustful of the world, and seemingly incapable of understanding what this kind of powerlessness feels like.

He also asks no questions about what abuse I might have experienced at the hands of a man.

Those who feel safe enough in their entitled righteousness to hurl hateful comments about women who come forward with reports of abuse at the hands of powerful men reinforce women's silence. We hear, "If it happened, why did she wait so long?" or, "Another woman looking for attention."

I'll give my father a pass given his generation, but why are women immediately assumed to be lying while men are always assumed to be telling the truth?

Women stay silent because we often see no other options.

It's part of our existence. It's been there, always. Felt, if not said. It is our safety. It was my safety. Or so I thought.

Perhaps I was wrong and silence protected me from nothing.

CHAPTER TWENTY-TWO
MOVING OUT

Tears choke me at odd moments, catching me off guard. They shouldn't. Any clear-thinking person whose heart beats would have expected at least a mini meltdown as I approach the date when I will to return to Florida to move out of our marital home. The condo is under contract with closing just days away, and there is packing and sorting and discarding to do.

As well as an excruciating goodbye.

The last two weeks have been a blur. My father went back to his home, convinced he could manage alone while I must occupy myself with the transactional realities of real estate sales and divorce proceedings and needing a new home myself. Guilt tugs at me. Although willing to drop everything if needed, my sister is three hours away from him; my brothers are even farther. All have the pull of their own families and their own jobs. But my trip can't be postponed.

There is no one who can be called in to separate my soon-to-be ex-husband's stuff from mine, no one else who can answer the questions: Do you want that vase we bought at that great gallery in Lenox? How about the juicer or the blender? No one else can ask, "Do you really want art I painted in your new house?"

Before facing the difficulties that await me in St. Pete, I take another short trip to Tucson, which leaves me flush with excitement and joy. This crazy idea of moving cross-country is now real and taking shape. I've found a house. The wreck of a home I first lusted over is unobtainable, the owners believing they will someday restore it themselves.

But a new oasis awaits me, a home that strikes my heart as I hit the slope of the driveway, open the gated entry, and step into the walled courtyard. It doesn't cry out for love with the same emptiness, but it does cry out, needing happiness to again fill its walls. It's not that the home has been unloved, quite the opposite. It's glorious underneath the clutter of a life deep in disarray. I stand in the courtyard feeling as though I've walked into a Tuscan villa. While exploring the ramada, the pool, the lush vegetation, and taking in the view of the mountains, a calm washes over me. I immediately imagine a life here, with love, all before I've even set foot inside its doors. The owner is selling as she too has experienced devastation at the hands of someone she loved who once loved her; the promise of her love and her life while in this house no longer exists. So like me, she must move on.

I walk inside to find soaring beamed ceilings, plaster walls, and polished concrete floors. The home is dark, cluttered, claustrophobic. It's been curtained off from the sun, from life, shutting out the world. An unintentional metaphor, I assume, for the state of the owner's life. The urge to fling open heavy drapes and shovel years of accoutrement into donation bags overwhelms me as I walk room to room with a secret smile I hide from the real estate agent. My metaphor is far more obvious. This is the house.

What would a therapist say about my penchant for the neglected home or a house long devoid of love? Why do I gravitate toward them and want to restore them? Why am I consumed with desire to fill these structures with the love that they have been missing? Clearly, something in my psyche is playing out, transferring what my heart feels into physical form.

Is this why I stayed in my marriage? Perhaps I have some unfulfilled psychological need around things or people lacking the love they deserve. I didn't see my husband as damaged when we married, nor understood the psychological source and depth of his alcoholism. It wasn't until after he became sober and his infidelity had become known, and after I had done enough therapy of my own, that I viewed him as empty. Confidence disguised his insecurity the way bravado does, falsely allowing those in the circle to see the shiny prism, but the crack in his identity lay buried deep inside. I don't know if any of his therapists drew the same conclusion, but I've come to view him as unconsciously believing that he was undeserving of love. Wouldn't that be the expected takeaway for a child who had been abandoned? He believed it under the surface, then simply proved it to himself with his behavior. "I don't deserve to be loved. Why else would my mother leave me? And this woman who claims to love me, she'll figure out one day that she is wrong, and she will leave too."

But why do I possess the desire to fix? And is *fix* the right word? Do I have an underlying desire to save or to fix, or is it simply that I can't fathom the idea of an incredible person or an incredible property lying fallow, unappreciated and missing one of the greatest gifts of humanity?

The power of love.

That night, I lie awake again, alone, in a bed that feels cavernous with loss, my heart branded with betrayal. In the morning, I'm to catch an early plane to meet the movers who will pack up that part of my life. Parting words worthy of the weight of this ending hijack my thoughts. Though it's been absent for long stretches, the anger has returned, and every ugly thing I never said ransacks me.

Wanting to shove the pain back down into its dormant state, I try to summon my obsession. I need him to help distract me with kind, hopeful words, to distract me with those intriguing eyes. But I can't hold him in my thoughts. The hurt of reality suppresses the fantasy.

The urge to lie to my husband and tell him I, too, had betrayed him slaps me again. The urge to tell him I hate him. The urge to accuse him of being incapable of love. The urge to tell him I still love him anyway. I can't settle on an approach. But this might be my last chance; it might be the last time we see each other. Whatever has been unsaid must be said now or forever held back. Now, with my strength building, my agency rebuilding—but not stable—I fear the moment will push me back, cause me to retreat into the old version of myself, the one who would hold back her truth. Like a newly poured foundation, the new me isn't yet set, hasn't been tested under duress. But are these urges about hurting him or saving myself? And are they constructive?

I fear the pendulum swing. I've seen it in women who were long constrained and are no longer willing to be. Women who rage and swear and openly flaunt their sexual desires, not because it is who they are but because the shackles are gone. Our models of female strength are confusing or hard to find or unassuming or just don't feel right. Historically, female fortitude has been thought of as a stoic front, resilience against the worst life throws at us. It's not a bad thing, but that's also an example of silence.

We've seen the pendulum swing in the business world for decades, particularly in male-dominated fields. Act like a man to get ahead. Play golf. Hold your booze. Use the word *fuck* as an adjective once in every sentence. Laugh at the endless sexual innuendo that is its own cover for inadequacy even when it makes your flesh crawl. It would be more accurate to say, act like the worst of men: bold, ugly, ruthless, selfish, arrogant.

I'm none of those things. I don't want to be those things. But what model of female strength feels honest and right for me?

And will I rest well if I leave him quietly? If I continue the good-girl behavior that I was trained in from birth?

Swallow your rage. Scuttle your dreams. Hold back your truth, your needs, your desires. Make yourself small. And don't dare talk about mistreatment at the hands of a man because you must have done something to provoke it.

These are the messages of femaleness. It's what we're taught in direct and indirect ways throughout our lives. Even when we intentionally break that chain or teach our daughters that they deserve better, the world shoves us back down. The reaction to an angry woman is judgment and criticism. We have been appointed as beings above that pettiness, held to a higher standard of calm, rational behavior that men are rarely expected to demonstrate.

I can't change the reality of misogyny, but I can change myself. I can find some way to thread this needle.

When my thoughts are clear, it's apparent that my hesitation is not about a ridiculous, irrational fear of saying tough things. I'm past that, I think. But I'm not past my own rational mind telling me whatever I feel the urge to say to my husband at this moment is pointless, the window of opportunity closed while I was buried in hurt and shock, unable to form coherent sentences, then attempting to rebuild from the ashes I'd been reduced to. Whatever I would say now would accomplish nothing and is therefore likely not worth the effort or the agony.

But isn't that also just like a woman? Often our inherent practicality shuts us down with thoughts of, *What's the point?*

Once I arrive in Florida, circumstances take the lead instead. My art studio is packed; the moving truck, loaded; my car, on a trailer. I return to our condo and crash on the sofa, my body forced to recharge. My husband, who has been conveniently away while I tend to my tasks, returns only thirty minutes before my cab is to arrive to take me back to the airport. I'm on the phone with my sister, who is taking a stint at Dad duty while I'm gone, and she's updating me on a new health issue he's facing.

My taxi has arrived, and I get a call that the car is waiting for me downstairs as I fill my husband in on my father's health. There is no time for the parting words I had contemplated in my head. No time for whatever parting words he wanted to share with me. For two days he has suggested that we have a meal together, a meal I couldn't fathom. I've seen the need for some kind of closure in his eyes, heard it in the urgency of his request, but my own turmoil prevented me from granting it. I gather my bags, and as I move toward the elevator, my throat clenches. I say the only thing I can think to say. The comment that has burned like an ember in me since I'd made the decision to leave.

"I hope they were all worth it."

He quickly chimes in. "No, they weren't. They weren't!" Tears spill down my face as the elevator doors close. Only when ensconced in the cab, does the next appropriate line slam into my head.

"Then you destroyed me for nothing."

CHAPTER TWENTY-THREE
I CAN'T SAVE ANOTHER MAN

My father has concluded I have a boyfriend. I learn this not from him but from my sister.

I'm on my way back to Wisconsin for more Dad duty after two weeks of travel. Halfway through my six-hour drive, I catch myself nodding off and pull off the highway for a power nap in a Starbucks parking lot. My body is telling me to stop, but that isn't possible. The long to-do list looms. The tactical, rational reality of what needs to be done supersedes the needs of my psyche.

After listening to my father complain of episodes of dizziness while I was attending to divorce business a week earlier, my sister and I collude and buy him a walker he does not want. She's thrown it in her car and driven three hours herself to deliver it. On arrival, she finds that Dad has been sitting in his recliner for days afraid to shower for fear of falling, and he has stubbornly refused to call his doctor.

We've come to a place where his identity and pride have slammed against the frailty of his body. Not trusting the emergency room after incorrect meds were given the last time, he refuses to let my sister take him there, preferring to wait another thirty-six hours until his cardiologist is available to chat by phone, only to be told to visit the emergency room anyway. After poking and prodding him for half a day, the medical staff determines dehydration is the cause. My father sits through several hours of IV hydration, arguing against the diagnosis as he "had a bottle of water yesterday."

Fifteen calls later, my sister and I have decided it's necessary to tag team "Dad watch" regardless of his ongoing insistence that he "can manage." We rearrange our lives, set aside our plans, and do what adult children do for elderly parents who've chosen to forgo plans of their own.

We become housekeepers, health monitors, worriers-in-chief. I'm driving up to relieve her, my immediate obligations covered, angry cat in tow. We spend a day together downloading before she must rush back to her teaching job and family. Our conversation becomes a circular debate filled with worry as we plot ways to convince a man of sound mind that his body is telling him it needs additional help, even if that sound mind would rather tough it out, deny, and not ask for help while his daughters imagine him dying alone on the floor. The worry isn't new. The resistance to help isn't new. Even this new dizziness has not shifted his self-assessment.

At five o'clock sharp, my sister and I arrive at our father's house for cocktail hour. I watch him shake as he hands me the glasses for ice, pours the whiskey, and drinks an old-fashioned—he never moves from his perch at the counter. He's jovial, but then, this isn't his first drink of the evening.

The walker sits just out of his reach but close enough that I know he's using it, and the tracks I see on the carpet confirm this. I dish up some soup—potato with bacon, a new staple—and leave the bowl in the microwave for him to heat up later as he's asked. After cocktails, my sister and I grab a quick dinner in town, then have the evening alone. Back at the lake house, we sit on the sofa until midnight, talking, trying to fill a little of the empty tank of sisterhood that COVID has drained, strategizing about how to handle Dad's current and future care. What is realistic? What help, if any, can we expect from our brothers? What's next?

This is when I learn that I must have a mystery boyfriend. Unable to comprehend my divorce years after the incidents that caused it, the pain I've carried since, or my decision to move to Tucson, my father has concocted the only explanation that seems logical to him. I'm running off with another man.

"Dad, you know what he did!" Kris tells me she responded to him.

"Yeah, but that was a while ago. I just don't understand," he replied.

Of course he doesn't understand. Conversation for him is a two-minute update of calendar events that stands in for real talk. Men from the John Wayne mold aren't known for their outward expressions of empathy or probing emotional questions. I've always known my father was proud of me; I've heard it in his voice as he talked about my life or my books with neighbors and friends. But he does not understand me.

He doesn't understand my preference for large, scary cities. My history of travel out of the country. My choice of strange foods like arugula and branzino when iceberg lettuce and frozen Swanson dinners would do. My history of remodeling perfectly serviceable homes. My decision to stay with a man who had betrayed me. My conflict over that decision. And he certainly doesn't understand my decision now to leave, alone, without another man as an impetus.

251

And he would never ask me why. Apparently, it's easier for him to assume I've been committing adultery. The thought makes me flinch.

No, he does not know me.

My sister doesn't say it as we sit with our wine, deep in the soul-healing conversation only sisters or best friends can provide, but I can hear the unspoken words flitting through her mind. I can see the question in her eyes. I can see the judgment. She doesn't say it aloud, but it's what I hear, or think I hear, nonetheless.

"What the hell took you so long? How could you have stayed?"

Or is the judgment my own projection?

Dad is drinking now. Drinking with his 11:30 a.m. lunch. Drinking on the days he must muster the energy to leave his recliner for a doctor's appointment. Another mid-afternoon, for no obvious reason. Then cocktail hour. Then, we learn, in the middle of the night.

His falls have become frequent affairs, usually in the early hours of the morning. He lies on the floor unable to get up, then crawls to his phone to find a neighbor he can wake to ask for help instead of his daughters. He refuses to call 911. He'll sleep on the floor until he can rouse a friend in the morning.

It's no longer safe for him to be alone. Finally, he can no longer lie to himself about his own fragile state. I make calls, schedule tours, and sort through the limited assisted-living options, but I know little about his financial situation. We ask him what he wants, getting only shrugs, blank stares, diversions, and a recitation of all the people he's known who have died in each facility. Listening for the thud or the crash that will tell her he's down, Kris spends the night in his tiny guest room steps from the kitchen. The room with a bed that feels like concrete with a picket fence headboard, duck art on every surface, and rifles in the closet.

I'm staying at the lake house and drive over in the morning. Frustration and lack of sleep are etched in her supremely patient face. Kris shoots wide eyes at me and shakes her head to signal it was bad. Once Dad is out of the room, she leans over and whispers that she heard him three times the previous night. Heard the clink of ice as it dropped into the glass. Heard the strike of wood as the liquor cabinet door closed. Heard him shuffle back to bed forty-five minutes later. Repeat. Eleven thirty, one thirty, three thirty.

When did this start? Why now? Is he self-medicating for pain or depression?

Kris frets, worried about his health, the effects of booze on his damaged heart and damaged lymph system, and how it interacts with his medications. She agonizes over what to say that will make him understand the consequences of this new behavior.

In other words, she's a newbie, applying logic to the illogical. I understand.

We sneak off to Dad's small concrete patio while he naps, and I listen as she quietly purges herself of the thoughts scrambling her mind. She's confused and just wants to make it stop, unable to add one more thing to the pile of things that have become unimaginable and intolerable. She wants to believe that there is some elusive argument that can talk sense into him if she could only figure out the proper words.

I sit, looking at her worried eyes, but can't form my own words. Instead, every raw, angry, frustrating, agonizing emotion I ever felt during my husband's active-addiction years washes over me like a tsunami, pulling memories I thought dormant to the surface as the wave retreats.

I can't save another man from himself. Not even if he is my father.

CHAPTER TWENTY-FOUR
CHOOSE BRAVERY

Excitement fills my heart as I stand in the driveway, keys to my new Tucson home in hand, waiting for the moving truck to arrive. Two months ago, my divorce was finalized, and I'm here at the precipice of my new life. My father has been reluctantly settled into a very nice assisted-living apartment, managing, for now, to accept the help that will ease our worry and his, even though he balks at the loss of autonomy. His friend Darlene is just one floor below, and they meet for cocktails in his room before dinner.

It's as close to being settled as I've been in more than a year. I wander the empty rooms, smiling, my shoes clicking on the polished concrete, considering where to place furniture. I try to remember what I have, as my things have been boxed and stored away for nearly a year. The home feels bigger and brighter and more hopeful than when I last saw it, the clutter of a confused, painful life now shed. Light streams across the plaster walls now that heavy curtains have been stripped from their rods, and I am in awe that this home is now mine.

I walk back outside to prop open the gate for the movers. A memory, an image, grips me. I step back ten feet and look again at the entrance to my home. Arched adobe brick. Generous vegetation. A deep blue sky with puffy clouds. Mountains in the distance.

It's the same image as the card from my tarot reading. The last card Amara pulled before announcing she saw me moving to the desert. I purchased the house shown on that card. Yes, as my realtor said to me after the complex process of closing the deal ended, this house was destined for me. Destined to bring happiness and abundance and contentment back into my life. I can feel it.

Although I've struggled endlessly with the question, "Why didn't I leave him then?" and have let that indecision and self-loathing leach life from me, I now know the answer: I could only make tough choices when I was emotionally ready to handle the uncertainty on the other side.

These days, I view the world through the lens of what addiction stole from my husband. What it stole from my marriage. What it stole from me. But that regret is waning.

Should I have seen it all coming? Seen the collapse of my marriage and my own self-respect for what it was as it played out? Probably. It seems clear in hindsight as I archive the events. But I also couldn't get out of my love bubble to see the entirety, to see the fragility of the threads as the tapestry was being woven. Marriage should include blind trust. A relationship knotted in suspicion is not worth having. But that also requires two people equally committed to honesty and respect.

In all reality, I suppose there are parts of me that didn't want to see it, didn't want his reality to be true. Instead, I performed my own compartmentalization. I found my own pretty little boxes where I could put my heart and my pride and my love to keep them intact.

Love is supposed to conquer all.

Do I regret my marriage? No.

Do I regret not leaving him the moment I learned the truth of his secrets? No. I don't regret that either because I needed to fight for that love. I needed to let our work at renewing what had been destroyed play out. I needed the painful, wrenching growth and to learn about myself. I needed to leave without hate and bitterness. I needed to leave knowing I had done—we had done—everything possible to try to salvage our love. I needed the time to begin to become the strong woman I see when I glimpse my future self.

I needed to become the woman who can now stand with the fear of my unknown and step into it anyway, even with a heart branded by betrayal.

As women reach the middle stage of our lives, we seem to share a collective experience, an experience seldom discussed or labeled as part of our development. A crisis, perhaps, that has been dismissed as another of those pesky hormonal emotional issues deemed too unimportant or boring to be analyzed by the people—let's just say it, the men—who do these things for a living or who provide the funding for psychological research. And without a profit motive, what would be the point? No neatly packaged product exists that will make it all better. Of course, the medical industry disagrees, wanting to sell us a pharmaceutical that will numb and distract. Anti-depressants, anyone?

But does that ever solve the core problem?

I'm talking about longing.

Longing in the broadest sense of the word. The craving for something distant, perhaps unobtainable, perhaps even unidentifiable. A missing element in our lives that we sometimes don't even know has left us, but we can feel that life has gone flat or seems less full of possibilities. We attribute that vague discontent to normal aging or an approaching "big birthday."

We've been caregivers. Relentlessly organizing the lives of our families, planning meals, carpooling, ensuring clean clothes for all, phoning the plumber when the kitchen sink backs up, checking on elderly parents and their meds and doctor appointments, squeezing juice out of the bank account when there is nothing but a dried, shriveled rind. Even when life has been free of crisis, we have, through necessity or choice, often set aside thoughts of our own needs. There has always been an electrician's bill to pay or kids needing help with algebra we barely remember, or the damn dog just peed on the carpet, again. With or without a job outside the home, regardless of our financial situations, our personal wants and needs and desires seem frivolous, too expensive right now, or simply not important enough to rise to the top of our priority list. *And we want regular orgasms too?*

There will be time for that later, we tell ourselves. Some day. This is the grand bargain we've made individually and with our families. Sometimes consciously, occasionally debated, and often simply assumed to be the nature of our roles as women.

It's assumed to be our identities. We are the givers. The caretakers. The glue of life. The fixers of things. We kiss the boo-boo, and magically everything is better.

In many ways, it is our strength. Women, by nature and nurture, are emotional custodians. Carriers and users of the genetic material that defines empathy. And for my money, the world would be a better place if empathy and decency influenced more decisions large and small.

But empathy can also be our downfall. Sometimes we give so much, for so long, that the well of our being runs dry. We live to care for others while only vaguely aware that there is nothing left in our tanks to fill us other than the fumes that were once dreams. Instead of children, we hover over grandchildren or retired husbands suffering their own identity crisis. We push even harder in our job because there are real needs, or we simply fill the day with nonsense tasks like finally scrubbing the tile grout in the kitchen with an old toothbrush and baking soda. Although oddly satisfying, returning the floor to its original color never returns us to our original state of hopes and dreams. It's simply a stand-in for the transformation often needed inside us.

We hear the word *self-care* bandied about in women's magazines and blogs and social media posts. We're told we need to remember to take time for ourselves. Take a walk and just breathe, go get that massage, find ten minutes to meditate, treat yourself to a new anti-wrinkle cream. While nice, these are only Band-Aids. They are diversionary tactics to make us feel that we've done something special for ourselves—given ourselves a treat. I'm not about to argue that a good skincare regime isn't worth investing in, God forbid, but its value is superficial. No professed miracle cream or serum can stop gravity, and it can't fill emptiness deep in our being. That problem won't be solved with a well-placed ad and forty dollars' worth of product.

Well, I hate to tell you ladies, but midlife *isn't* later. It's now.

We wake up one day and realize the children are gone or our parents are gone and suddenly there are fewer demands on our time. If we're particularly self-aware, we recognize there are no longer any excuses for not doing the things we've always told ourselves we would, or we realize that time is running short. Sometimes those desires are secret, never-uttered wants, sometimes they're an interest set aside years ago due to time or finances, sometimes they are a vague sense of something missing we can't quite pinpoint, and sometimes, they boldly jump up and bite us in the ass, refusing to be ignored.

A crash, a crisis, a breakdown.

Regardless, we dismiss them at our peril. The choice is to act or to spend the balance of our lives regretting what we did not do. And it *is* a choice whether recognized as such or not.

For many, that choice is to finally say no to demands others make on us, to read the unread books stacked up on the shelf, to finally take that painting class we've always dreamed of but never deemed important. For others, its time spent with girlfriends or travel or charity work or a new job. For others still, it's to take a lover or to make the difficult choice to walk away from a relationship that no longer serves them.

The choice needn't be big or externally dramatic. It can be as simple as questioning your own needs for the first time in years.

Ladies, this is part of the reckoning of our middle years. The necessary question: What do *I* want in my life for this next stage, however long or short that may be?

And the learning is in the questioning.

The answer comes easily for some as nothing more than a readjustment of attitude and time. For others, the answer agonizing and fraught with hours of therapy and months or even years of exploration and indecision. Regardless, sooner or later, the unmet need, if it exists, must be addressed or it will fester. Without the busyness of family demands, longing and unmet needs will haunt us even if we choose to suppress them, even if we call them by another name, even if we continue to convince ourselves they are not worthy of exploring. They will be there under the surface, poking up for a breath now and then.

What will you do when those moments come? Lie to yourself? Rationalize and suppress yet again? Stay in the shadows? Or will you find your bravery and seek out joy, contentment, renewed desire, and longing?

I choose bravery. In that choice is my belief that the rest will follow. As my husband said to me on our first date, "You deserve to be happy."

He was right all along.

ACKNOWLEDGMENTS

I never imagined I would write this book. I never imagined I *could* write this book. I never imagined I would *need* to write this book. But a NEED it did become.

I began by journaling as a supplement to therapy. And the more those painful, unformed, agonizing thoughts spilled onto the page, the more I thought of my mother and my sister. Women who sat with regret at the end of their lives for things not done. The more I wrote, the more I thought of the women I've known who've held their pain inside believing silence was protection. I thought of the women I've met who set aside their needs for others believing one day it would be their turn. These are the reasons I wrote this book. I wrote for the women who have, or are, suffering in silence.

I wrote because to not write this book would be another silencing of me.

The handful of people I invited into my vulnerability circle are people I hold forever in my debt. You heard my voice break and tremble as I spoke about parts of my story. You heard my tears over the phone as I re-lived moments of my life. You've sat patiently holding me in your thoughts when I couldn't speak the details of my pain. And you've been my support, believing that the rawness and vulnerability of my words would find their way into the hearts of others.

My undying thanks to the best book cheerleader ever, Richelle Fredson. Your words of encouragement and confidence in me have kept me going even when my body was telling me to hide under the bed and forget this big scary thing.

To my publishing group, Naren Aryal, Jess Cohn, Dayna Jackson, and Lauren Magnussen, thank you for your confidence, professionalism, and enthusiasm. You've been a delight to work with. I couldn't have had a better team.

To my sister Kris Hackl, you're the best. I imagine there are things in this book that will surprise you, things I didn't speak of. But it wasn't you, it was my fears. I know you're always there.

To my dear friend Ann Chikahisa, you're the first person I think of when I need to cry or to scream with joy. I know you're there always, in all things. But I'm sorry, I still won't tell you who my obsession is, so you can stop trying to get me drunk.

To my boys, I'm so sorry that you needed to hear the truth, finally. It's hard. It hurts. But truth, even the most painful of truth, is necessary. It's okay to still love Dad. I want that for you.

I also want to thank my former husband. I know this isn't what you would expect of me, and you won't read this book, but I thank you, nonetheless. Not for the pain you inflicted on me. Not for the emptiness inside you that couldn't believe you deserved my love. I thank you because you showed me my capacity for love. I thank you because I've become a woman who could write this book and speak her truth. However painful, I'm better on the other side.

ABOUT THE AUTHOR

Growing up in Wisconsin, Dana Killion developed a curiosity for the world beyond the confines of small-town life, finding inspiration in the intrepid explorer, Nancy Drew. Dana's thirst for more exhilarating pastures led to a career in the apparel industry, and eventually, back to her love of story. She created a mystery series based on the long-lived desire to shed light on shadows. The series renders a journey through crime and corruption countered by her protagonist's ability to confront deceit.

Now, Dana presents her first memoir. A story born of a life in turmoil, a situation where the only way through was to write it. And as she wrote, the themes in her personal trauma became clear and loud and screamed for attention because they are the themes of many women, not just women with an addict in her life, but women who have been silent and who have set aside their truth for the benefit of another. Women ready to find the strength and solace Dana has found through her own re-invention.

Dana currently resides in Tucson, Arizona with her kitty, Isabel, happily avoiding snow and mending her heart.